Cataloging
U.S.A.

Cataloging
U.S.A.

By Paul S. Dunkin

American Library Association
Chicago

International Standard Book Number 0-8389-0071-2 (1969)

Library of Congress Catalog Card Number 69-17830

Copyright © 1969 by the American Library Association

Printed in the United States of America

Second Printing, December 1970

To Tommy

Preface

CATALOGING U.S.A. is not a how-to-do-it book. It is a why-do-it book. That fact determines the book's audience, its purpose, and its scope.

The beginning student of cataloging who learns the rules but is not content mechanically to apply them—I write for him. The experienced cataloger who seeks to think about his job—I write for him. The public service librarian who is not certain what he should find in the catalog and how he should interpret the catalog to its user—I write for him. The library administrator who wonders what he should expect of his catalog department or of a cataloging service he is about to buy—I write for him. These are my audience.

The purpose of this book, then, is not to list facts and techniques with elaborate sets of examples. Instead, it proposes to examine attitudes toward techniques and toward what seem to be facts. "Why do it?" The answer can be only opinions—my opinions.

Cataloging, like all library work, is a pragmatic business. Here are the books. Since Gutenberg they have been pouring into libraries. What to do with them? Anything. Anything to get them out of the way before the next heap of books is dumped at the library's door. Anything to make it easy to find them again if they are needed. Now "anything" quickly becomes habit if it seems to work, and men and libraries grow old doing the same "anything." They even think up reasons for having done it, and they tell themselves they did it because of the reasons. And thus "anything" becomes at last hallowed tradition.

But we cannot accept and defend any process simply because it has always been done that way. We can hope to be good catalogers (just as we can hope to be good librarians in any other area) only if we look always for the real reasons for what we do, and if we ask if these reasons are good. This is not all. We have the right to find fault only if we also try to think of a better way to do the job. We can be good catalogers only if we are skeptics; but we must be creative skeptics.

This book, I repeat, will not tell you how to do anything. Yet, in a sense, it *is* a how-to-do-it book. It tells you: Ask "Why?" every step of the way. Ask "Why?" even of my opinions.

The book deals almost entirely with theory and principles. Only now and then, if it seems necessary to a complete understanding of the implications of theory, is some detail of practice briefly described.

It follows that the work is not a substitute for rules of entry and description, subject headings rules and lists, classification schemes, or other similar reference books. Instead, it is only a commentary on such works, and it does not profess to comment on more than a few of what seem to be the most important aspects of each.

Comments are made only on cataloging in the United States. Many interesting practices have always been part of cataloging abroad. But to write of these practices also would have taken several books. This work looks at the foreign scene only when it seems necessary to understand fully some procedure in this country. If a reader in some other country finds anything in this book helpful, that will be, I hope, good for him and for his country's cataloging. I am not at all sure, however, that what we do and think in this country will be of value in other countries with other conditions. In no sense is this a book of American intellectual imperialism.

Cataloging in the United States derives from Cutter. A study of the theory and principles of American cataloging is largely a study of the theory and principles of Cutter and what we have done with them. I have written this book at a time when Cutter's dictionary card catalog is still the typical general library catalog. I have written also in a time of change; but in many ways the change has not yet gone beyond experimentation. The literature of Documentation, Information Science, and Automation is voluminous, and its content and attitudes differ from day to day. The only realistic base from which to work seemed to be this ancient tool, the dictionary card catalog. It is not impossible that whatever may replace the dictionary card catalog will have to answer our doubts and questions about the basic principles of that catalog.

It remains to express my appreciation of all who took time to read this book in manuscript and to offer criticisms and suggestions:

Esther Piercy, Phyllis Richmond, Laura Colvin, and the (to me) anonymous readers to whom the American Library Association Publishing Department sent the manuscript. I have given careful thought to all their ideas, even though I have not always carried them out. Finally, Pauline Love has been a patient and thoughtful editor.

PAUL S. DUNKIN

Contents

A Few Books about Cataloging   xv

1. Mr. Cutter's Catalog   1

Form of the Catalog   1
Arrangement of the Catalog   3
The Individual Code   4
Cutter: The General Code   5
Objects and Means   6
Convenience of the Public   7
Rules for a Printed Dictionary Catalogue   7

2. The Prophet and the Law: Codes after Cutter   9

The Anglo-American Code of 1908 (ALA 1908)   9
Prussian Instructions (PI)   11
ALA Draft, 1941 (ALA 1941)   11
Osborn's "Crisis"   12
LC Studies of Descriptive Cataloging   13
Interlude: The Vatican Code of 1948   13
ALA-LC Codes, 1949 (ALA 1949 and LC 1949)   14
Seymour Lubetzky   15
The Paris Statement: October 1961 (Paris 1961)   17
Anglo-American Code, 1967 (ALA 1967): Compromise   17
ALA 1967: Conclusion   18
The COSATI Standard   19
Subject Headings and Classification   20
The Prophet and the Law   21

3. Who Did It? Author and Title Entry and Heading   23

What Is an Author?   24
Heading   27
The Two Objectives   27
Author Headings   28
Interlude on Evidence   30
Rigid and Relaxed: Conclusion   31
Headings for Anonymous Works   32
Arbitrary Entry   33
Books with More than One Author   34
Books Whose Authors Change   35
Serials   36
Catalogers' Convention: The Non-Author Heading   40
    Pseudo-Author Headings   41
    "Institution" Headings   41
    Form Headings   43
    Certain Religious Works   44
Main Entry and Added Entry   44
Who Did It? Short End to a Long Chapter   46

4. What Does It Look Like? Descriptive Cataloging   48

The Two Objectives   49
But How Brief?   50
Title and Edition   51
The Two Objectives Again   53
The Imprint   55
The Collation   57
The Notes   61
The Tracing   62
Serials   62
Brevity Is the Soul of Wit   64

5. What Is It About? Subject Entry   65

Cutter   66
The Two Objectives   66
Specific Entry   67
Direct and Specific Subject Headings   69
    Single-Noun Heading   70
    Compound Heading   70
Subdivision (Cutter)   71
Subdivision (Haykin)   73

Subdivision: Persons and Places 75
   Persons 76
   Places 76
Subdivision: Duplicate Entry 78
The Third Objective 79
Cutter and Haykin: Summary 81
The Subject Heading List 82
The Alphabetico-Classed Catalog 84
The Noun Approach (Schwartz and Cutter) 87
The Noun Approach (Prevost) 88
The Noun Approach (Others) 91
The Non-Subject Heading 94
What Is the Book About? 95

6. Where Does It Go? Call Numbers 96

The Two Objectives 96
Fixed Location 97
Relative Location 98
Dewey Decimal Classification (DDC) 98
Interlude: Cutter's Expansive Classification (EC) 100
Library of Congress Classification (LCC) 101
Classification of What? 103
Notation 106
Bias 107
Change 108
Reclassification 112
The Second Objective Again 112
Serials 115
How To Find the Call Number 116
Book Numbers 122
Panacea 123
Reader Interest Classification (RIC) 124
The Bibliographic Classification (BC) 126
International Classification (IC) 128
From Book to Microthought 130
Colon Classification (CC) 131
Universal Decimal Classification (UDC) 135
Where Does the Book Go? 137

7. Mr. Cutter's Catalog: Today and Tomorrow 138

Rules and Classification 138
Duality of the Two Objectives 139

The Public   140
Dilemma   142
Dilemma—Parallel?   143
Jewett   144
Library of Congress   144
Centralized and/or Commercial Processing   147
The Machine   149
The Book Catalog   149
Cutter's Tomorrow   151
Finally: The Cataloger's Tomorrow   152
Proteus   153

Index   155

A Few Books about Cataloging

In no sense does this pretend to be a complete bibliography; it is not even a complete list of all books referred to in the following pages. It is truly only what it is called. These books are basic books or examples of types of books of which no cataloger can afford to be ignorant.

Arrangement under each topic is chronological. Unless otherwise indicated, later references to these books will be simply by their authors' surnames.

GENERAL

The Past

There is no satisfactory general history of cataloging. The following books deal with certain aspects of that history.

U.S. Bureau of Education. *Public Libraries in the United States of America: Their History, Condition, and Management.* Washington: Govt. Print. Off., 1876. Part I has been reprinted by the University of Illinois Graduate School of Library Science as No. 4 of its Monograph Series (1964). The 4th ed. of Part II, Cutter's *Rules for a Printed Dictionary Catalogue,* has been reprinted by the Library Association. Part I is referred to as *Public Libraries.*

Norris, Dorothy May. *A History of Cataloguing and Cataloguing Methods 1100–1850, with an Introductory Survey of Ancient Times.* London: Grafton & Co., 1939.

In spite of its title, this book deals chiefly with the English scene. It is largely annalistic, sometimes not too scholarly, and there is little attempt at interpretation. Among its useful features are the lengthy extracts from many catalogs, chiefly medieval, given by way of illustration for the text.

Strout, Ruth French. "The Development of the Catalog and Cataloging Codes," in her *Toward a Better Cataloging Code*, p.4–25. Chicago: Univ. of Chicago Graduate Library School, 1957.

This is a better balanced and more interpretative account than Norris, but, of course, briefer and narrower in its interest.

Ranz, Jim. *The Printed Book Catalog in American Libraries: 1723–1900.* ("ACRL Monograph," No.26) Chicago: American Library Assn., 1964.

Unlike the Norris book, this is much more than its title implies. Ranz does, indeed, deal admirably with the printed book catalog in its early form, but perhaps even more important is his account of the development of cataloging theory in this country as the various catalogs were compiled and printed.

The Present

Osborn, Andrew D. *Serial Publications: Their Place and Treatment in Libraries.* Chicago: American Library Assn., 1955.

A thought-provoking study of practice in the mid-fifties, this book is still valuable.

Jackson, Sidney L. *Catalog Use Study;* ed. by Vaclav Mostecky. Chicago: American Library Assn., 1958.

This study struggles with a mass of statistics from a number of different kinds of libraries. Its conclusions seldom differ from those of earlier studies, but it is the most ambitious attempt yet to describe that intangible: the user of the American general library catalog.

Jolley, Leonard. *The Principles of Cataloguing.* London: Crosby Lockwood & Son Ltd., 1960.

This is a sometimes stimulating study from the English-Australian point of view, written while work on the *Anglo-American Cataloging Rules* was still in process and while Seymour Lubetzky was still editor.

Library of Congress. *The Cataloging-in-Source Experiment,* Washington: Library of Congress, 1960.

This is a detailed, carefully documented account of a plan for printing catalog information on the verso of the title page or elsewhere in the book.

Piercy, Esther J., and Talmadge, Robert, issue eds. *Cooperative and Centralized Cataloging, Library Trends,* 16, No.1 (July 1967).

A useful collection of papers about a problem still in a state of flux.

The Future

King, G. W., and others. *Automation and the Library of Congress.* Washington: Library of Congress, 1963.

Strout, Ruth French, ed. *Library Catalogs: Changing Dimensions.* Chicago and London: Univ. of Chicago Pr., 1964. Also published as *Library Quarterly,* 34, No.1 (Jan. 1964).

Obviously the LC automation study is not about cataloging only, but it may greatly affect cataloging. The papers, edited by Strout, were presented at the annual conference of the Graduate Library School, University of Chicago, August 5–7, 1963, and examine current changes in our notions of the form and functions of the catalog. These two books are, of course, simply an introduction to the host of books and articles the cataloger must read if he is to be kept informed.

Author and Title Entry and Description

Codes Compiled by Individual Authors

Panizzi, Sir Anthony, and others. "Rules for the Compilation of the Catalogue," in *Catalogue of Printed Books in the British Museum*, Vol. I, p.v–ix. London: Printed by Order of the Trustees, 1841.

Compiled by Panizzi, Thomas Watts, J. Winter Jones, J. H. Parry, and Edward Edwards, these famous ninety-one rules had a profound influence on the development of American cataloging codes.

Jewett, Charles C. *Smithsonian Report on the Construction of Catalogues of Libraries, and Their Publication by Means of Separate, Stereotyped Titles. With Rules and Examples.* 2d ed. Washington: The Smithsonian Institution, 1853; reprinted, Ann Arbor, Mich.: University Microfilms, Inc., 1961.

The rules lean heavily on Panizzi. Perhaps much more notable than the rules is the first American proposal to catalog a book only one time, with other libraries using a copy of this entry for their copy of the book.

Cutter, Charles A. *Rules for a Dictionary Catalog.* 4th ed., rewritten; Washington: Govt. Print. Off., 1904; republished, London: The Library Association, 1953.

The first edition, *Rules for a Printed Dictionary Catalogue*, appeared in 1876 as Part II of the U.S. Bureau of Education *Public Libraries in the United States*. Probably more than any other single work Cutter's *Rules* has influenced the philosophy, form, and development of the catalog in American general libraries. Unless stated otherwise, all references to Cutter's *Rules* are to the fourth edition, 1904.

ALA-LC Codes

American Library Association. *Catalog Rules: Author and Title Entries.* American ed. Chicago: ALA, 1908. Referred to as ALA 1908.

American Library Association. *A.L.A. Catalog Rules: Author and Title Entries.* Preliminary American 2d ed. Chicago: ALA, 1941. Referred to as ALA 1941.

American Library Association. *A.L.A. Cataloging Rules for Author and Title Entries.* 2d ed. Clara Beetle, ed. Chicago: ALA, 1949. Referred to as ALA 1949.

Library of Congress. *Rules for Descriptive Cataloging in the Library of Congress; Adopted by the American Library Association.* Washington: Library of Congress, 1949. Referred to as LC 1949.

Cataloging Rules of the American Library Association and the Library of

Congress; Additions and Changes 1949–1958. Washington: Library of Congress, 1959.

Lubetzky, Seymour. *Code of Cataloging Rules . . . Prepared for the Catalog Code Revision Committee . . . With an Explanatory Commentary* by Paul Dunkin. Chicago: American Library Assn., 1960. Referred to as Lubetzky 1960.

American Library Association, Library of Congress, Library Association, and Canadian Library Association. *Anglo-American Cataloging Rules.* North American Text. Chicago, ALA, 1967. Referred to as ALA 1967. The British Text (London: The Library Assn., 1967) is referred to as LA 1967.

Some Modern Non-American Codes

The Prussian Instructions: Rules for the Alphabetical Catalogs of the Prussian Libraries; tr. from 2d ed., authorized Aug. 10, 1908, by Andrew D. Osborn. Ann Arbor: Univ. of Michigan Pr., 1938. Referred to as PI.

The Vatican Library. *Rules for the Catalog of Printed Books;* tr. from 2d Italian ed. by Thomas J. Shanahan, Victor A. Schaefer, Constantin T. Vesselowsky. Wyllis E. Wright, ed. Chicago: American Library Assn., 1948.

Criticism, Interpretation, Etc.

Osborn, Andrew D. *The Crisis in Cataloging.* n.p., American Library Institute, 1941. Also published in *Library Quarterly,* 11:393–411 (Oct. 1941).

This pamphlet marked the beginning of an age and gave a name to that age.

Library of Congress. *Studies of Descriptive Cataloging.* Washington: Govt. Print. Off., 1946. Referred to as LC *Studies.*

This book opened a new and drastic approach to elaborate description. Its theory is sound both when tested by logic and when tested by experiment. We have not yet fully achieved the brevity and simplicity in description which it showed is possible and worthwhile.

Lubetzky, Seymour. *Cataloging Rules and Principles: A Critique of the A.L.A. Rules for Entry and a Proposed Design for Their Revision.* Washington: Library of Congress, 1953. Referred to as Lubetzky Report.

What the LC *Studies* had done for description, this book did for author and title entry. As with the LC *Studies,* the goals of simplicity Lubetzky set for us have not yet been fully achieved.

Ranganathan, S. R. *Headings and Canons: Comparative Study of Five Catalogue Codes.* Madras: S. Viswanathan; London: G. Blunt and Sons, 1955.

This book helps to provide an understanding of American cataloging ferment in the forties and fifties against the background of the world scene. Perhaps there is too much emphasis on Ranganathan's own code, but this is one of his most clearly written books, with little resort to jargon.

Strout, Ruth French, ed. *Toward a Better Cataloging Code*. Chicago: Univ. of Chicago Graduate Library School, 1957. Also published as *Library Quarterly*, 26, No.4 (Oct. 1956).

These papers, presented at the annual conference of the Graduate Library School, June 13–15, 1956, mark the first of a series of conferences and institutes which studied the problems of catalog code revision. Others were held at Stanford (1958), Montreal (1960), and Paris (1961).

International Federation of Library Associations. *International Conference on Cataloguing Principles, Paris, 9th–18th October, 1961: Report;* A. H. Chaplin, ed. London: 1963.

This was the last of the conferences on catalog code revision. It grew out of the American code revision then in progress, and its Statement of Principles is, perhaps, the best account of the hopes of that revision. Statement of Principles referred to as Paris Statement 1961.

Subject Headings

Rules

Rules for subject headings were published as part of the various editions of Cutter's *Rules for a Dictionary Catalog*, the Vatican Library *Rules for the Catalog of Printed Books*, and in the introductory material of various editions of Sears's *List of Subject Headings*.

Lists

The two basic lists of subject headings used in American general libraries have long been the Library of Congress list, directed toward the needs of large research libraries, and the Sears list, for smaller libraries. Each exists in several editions, and also there have been a number of lists compiled for special needs. It seems unnecessary to describe specific editions of any at this point.

Criticism, Interpretation, Etc.

Prevost, Marie Louise. "An Approach to Theory and Method in General Subject Heading," *Library Quarterly*, 16:140–51 (April 1946).

This, of course, is not a book, and it had little or no influence. But it combines a thoughtful and thought-provoking attack on a basic problem of American subject heading practice with a drastic proposed solution.

Pettee, Julia. *Subject Headings: The History and Theory of the Alphabetical Subject Approach to Books*. New York: H. W. Wilson Company, 1947.

A comprehensive but somewhat conservative study, this book is still useful.

Haykin, David Judson. *Subject Headings: A Practical Guide.* Washington: Govt. Print. Off., 1951.

An attempt to present Library of Congress practice in an orderly manner and to offer rationalization for that practice, Haykin's work shows how little real change there has been since Cutter.

Tauber, Maurice F., ed. *Subject Analysis of Library Materials.* New York: Columbia University School of Library Service, 1953.

These papers, presented June 24–28, 1952, at an institute sponsored by the Columbia School of Library Service and the American Library Association Division of Cataloging and Classification, offer a useful interpretative statement of the then current practice and criticism of classification, subject headings, and user approach.

Coates, E. J. *Subject Catalogues: Headings and Structure.* London: The Library Assn., 1960.

Although basically British in attitude, this book is of considerable value for its rather logical study of Cutter, its account of what has happened to subject headings since Cutter, and its suggested solutions.

CLASSIFICATION

Schedules

The following classification schemes will be considered in Chapter 6 in some detail. Some exist in many editions; it seems unnecessary to describe specific editions of any at this point.

Dewey Decimal Classification. Referred to as DDC with number of edition added, e.g., DDC 17 for the 17th ed.

Expansive Classification. Referred to as EC.

Library of Congress Classification. Referred to as LCC.

Reader Interest Classification. Referred to as RIC.

Bibliographic Classification. Referred to as BC.

International Classification. Referred to as IC.

Colon Classification. Referred to as CC. All references are to the 6th ed. New York: Asia Publishing House, 1960.

Universal Decimal Classification. Referred to as UDC.

Criticism, Interpretation, Etc.

The titles one could list here are legion; what follows tries only to be representative.

Kelley, Grace O. *The Classification of Books: An Inquiry into its Usefulness to the Reader.* New York: H. W. Wilson Company, 1938.

This is an admirable book.

Merrill, William S. *Code for Classifiers.* 2d ed. Chicago: American Library Assn., 1939.

A collection of rules for traditional American library classification with some discussion of each, the work is often arbitrary; now out of date.

Sayers, W. C. Berwick. *A Manual of Classification*. 3d ed., rev. London: Grafton & Co., 1955. Referred to as Sayers. The 4th ed., rev. and partly rewritten by Arthur Maltby (London: Andre Deutsch, 1967), is referred to as Sayers-Maltby.

Here is a sound statement of the older British theoretical (as opposed to the American practical) approach to library classification.

Shera, Jesse H., and Egan, Margaret E. *The Classified Catalog: Basic Principles and Practices*. Chicago: American Library Assn., 1956.

This is an excellent book about a kind of library catalog seldom seen in this country.

Eaton, Thelma, and Strout, Donald E., eds. *The Role of Classification in the Modern American Library*. Champaign, Ill. Illini Union Bookstore, 1959.

In these papers of the Allerton Park Institute, November 1–4, 1959, there is confrontation of modern theory of classification with traditional American library classification.

Mills, Jack. *A Modern Outline of Library Classification*. 2d impr. London: Chapman & Hall, 1960.

This is a useful book, once the reader masters the tiny type. It is a thoughtful sketch of the modern theoretical approach to library classification. British, occasionally ponderous and pontifical, it is best read in connection with Palmer's *Itself an Education*.

LaMontagne, Leo E. *American Library Classification with Special Reference to the Library of Congress*. Hamden, Conn.: Shoe String Pr., 1961.

The historical section of this curious book is annalistic and rambling, but the section describing the development and content of the various schedules of the Library of Congress Classification is quite useful.

Palmer, Bernard I. *Itself an Education: Six Lectures on Classification*. London: The Library Assn., 1962.

Intended to accompany study of Mills's *Modern Outline*, this book is lucid, literate, and sometimes witty.

Dewey, Melvil. Introduction to the 12th ed., reprinted in his *Dewey Decimal Classification and Relative Index*, Vol. I, p.63–108. 17th ed. Lake Placid Club, N.Y.: Forest Press, Inc., 1965.

This is a vigorously written statement of the founder's ideas and attitudes.

Custer, Benjamin A. Editor's Introduction, in Melvil Dewey, *Dewey Decimal Classification and Relative Index*, Vol. I, p.5–61. 17th ed. Lake Placid Club, N.Y.: Forest Press, Inc., 1965.

Custer sketches the history of efforts to keep DDC up to date. The new features of the seventeenth edition are described, and some of the plans for future editions are mentioned.

Schimmelpfeng, Richard H., and Cook, C. Donald, eds. *The Use of the Library of Congress Classification*: Proceedings of the Institute on the Use of the Library of Congress Classification sponsored by the American Library Association Resources and Technical Services Division,

Cataloging and Classification Section, New York City, July 7–9, 1966. Chicago: ALA, 1968.

PERIODICALS

Journal of Cataloging and Classification, 1948–56.

The journal is a monument to the enthusiasm and persistence of Marie Louise Prevost, without whose dogged belief in the need for a journal it might never have been. Many of the articles are dated, but some are timeless.

Serial Slants, 1950–56.

Some valuable ideas about serials problems appeared inside its covers.

Library Resources and Technical Services, 1957–date.

After the reorganization of ALA and the creation of the Resources and Technical Services Division, *Serial Slants* and *Journal of Cataloging and Classification* merged. The journal thus founded was *Library Resources and Technical Services.* Its excellence, like that of *Journal of Cataloging and Classification,* is due to the imaginative editing of Esther J. Piercy.

Articles on cataloging and classification may be found also in some more general periodicals such as: *American Documentation, College and Research Libraries, Special Libraries, Library Journal, Library Quarterly,* and *Library Trends.*

1

Mr. Cutter's Catalog

Charles A. Cutter's *Rules for a Printed Dictionary Catalogue* first appeared in 1876 and the fourth and final edition in 1904. This remarkable book did not, like Athene, spring full-grown from the head of Zeus. It grew out of man's experience over many centuries in the making of catalogs. It grew out of Cutter's own experience in the making of catalogs, particularly his experience with his great dictionary catalog of the Boston Athenaeum. It grew out of Cutter's thoughtful study of catalogs made by his contemporaries and of their theories and principles.

A wide-ranging, creative, open mind is at work on every page of Cutter's *Rules*. Above all, a modern mind. Cutter did not anticipate our jargon, but he did anticipate many of the problems we describe with that jargon. Probably his is the only book of rules for cataloging which is fascinating reading.

Many things go into the making of a catalog. We shall look briefly at a few of them and Cutter's attitude toward each.

Form of the Catalog

Men made their first catalogs as they made their first books, by hand. Indeed, the catalogs were themselves books or parts of books. The clay tablets of Sumer (ca. 2000 B.C.), the Pinakes of Callimachus (ca. 250 B.C.), the "Seven Summaries" of Liu Hain (ca. A.D. 20), the catalogs of medieval monasteries—these are but samples of the many handmade catalogs of handmade books. Like everything else touched by the hand of man, they show an infinite variety.

The invention of printing was the invention of mass production of manuscripts. Almost at once we needed more catalogs because there

1

were many more books and, as a result, more libraries. But printing carried a built-in solution: the printed catalog. For printing, like many another invention, was only the work of the hand made faster and easier. And, just as the catalog of handmade books had been itself a handmade book, so the catalog of printed books was for centuries often itself a printed book.

We changed from printed catalogs to card catalogs for at least two reasons:

First, libraries grow. The moment one new book comes to the library the printed catalog of that library is out of date. Thus the history of cataloging in any library which lasted for some years is the history of that library's printed catalog, its successive supplements, and, finally, brand-new editions. The printed catalog and its supplements can deal—awkwardly it is true—with steady growth; an unexpected growth is another matter. The French Revolution, for instance, abruptly added to the national property the royal library, the libraries of the religious and lay corporations, and the libraries of the émigrés. A flood of books swept into the older libraries which did survive and into newly established libraries. How could they be organized quickly and efficiently? What may have been the first card catalog—written on playing cards—was the answer proposed. The supplements to a printed catalog were often printed from card catalogs of additions; to use a card catalog from the very beginning was a logical next step. Not merely does the card catalog respond quickly to growth; unlike the printed catalog, it demands that the user look in only one alphabet for all books no matter how recently they came into the library.

Second, in 1901 the Library of Congress (LC) began to sell its printed cards to libraries "on such liberal terms," wrote Cutter (p.5), "that any new library would be foolish not to make its catalog mainly of them." After all, as Cutter noted, this would save the cataloger's time for other things.

The first edition of Cutter's rules (1876) bore the title *Rules for a Printed Dictionary Catalogue*; but the last edition (1904) carried a note that these rules "written primarily for a printed catalog, have been enlarged in this fourth edition to include the needs of a card catalog" (p.24). The printed catalog continues to influence our thinking even when we work with card catalogs. For instance, we talk of the "main entry" for a book even though (if we use printed cards or perhaps if we use typed cards) every card for that book is exactly alike. Apparently the notion that there is a "main entry" comes from definitions such as that by Cutter (p.21) in which the "main entry" in a printed catalog is said to be "the full or principal entry" because this entry supplies contents and notes which may be omitted in other entries of the book under such things as subject or title.

Arrangement of the Catalog

Broadly speaking, there are two basic approaches to the arrangement of catalogs: the classed and the alphabetical. The classed catalog is arranged by the logic of a classification scheme, and this scheme may deal only with broad general classes, or it may subdivide its classes very minutely. The classed catalog is probably the older, beginning with catalogs which simply listed books in the subject sequence by which they had been shelved. The alphabetical catalog has the simple but illogical arrangement of the alphabet.

Neither approach necessarily means that the catalog is a single list; the catalog may, indeed, be divided into two or more lists. A classed catalog may also have an index or indexes of such things as specific subjects, authors, titles, and forms. Likewise an alphabetical catalog by authors may have an index or indexes of such things as specific subjects, titles, and forms.

Nor are the two approaches mutually exclusive. The alphabetico-classed catalog, for instance, consists of alphabetically arranged broad subjects, each subdivided alphabetically into its parts and subparts. This arrangement also may have an index or indexes by such things as authors, titles, and forms; or it may interfile all these elements with the alphabetico-classed headings.

The dictionary catalog unites in one single alphabetical sequence authors, titles, specific subjects, and forms. It does not require any separate indexes. "The author- and subject-catalogue may be kept separate or mixed in one alphabet . . . For the dictionary system one alphabet is decidedly to be preferred . . . Yet there is the slight disadvantage that the mind is diverted from its object by the presence of headings of other kinds than the one wanted; title- and subject-headings especially interfering with one another," wrote Cutter in *Public Libraries* (p.552). This "slight disadvantage" grows as the collection and its catalog grow; in recent years the divided catalog has become rather popular.

Combinations of these approaches seem almost infinite, and catalogers have experimented and argued endlessly over the virtues of each possibility. Jim Ranz has an excellent account of the experiments in arrangement in this country 1850–75 (p.55–75).

Cutter developed and refined the dictionary catalog arrangement in his monumental catalog of the Boston Athenaeum and in his *Rules*; and the cards that the Library of Congress began to issue in 1901 were cards for a dictionary catalog. The dictionary catalog can be used easily and efficiently by anyone familiar with the alphabet. It has dominated American cataloging ever since.

The Individual Code

Early catalogs dealt generally with small collections, and they were compiled largely by people working more or less independently. The cataloger of each collection set up his own code unless, of course, he was content to follow the rules already in use in some other library. This procedure was generally followed down to the middle of the nineteenth century, and many useful catalogs were produced under this rugged individualism, e.g., Hyde's catalog of the Bodleian Library (1674) or Poole's catalog of the Boston Mercantile Library (1854).

Yet the uses of standardization must have been known rather early too. For instance, the thirteenth-century union list of monastery library holdings, the *Registrum Librorum Angliae,* and its continuation by John Boston of Bury about 1410, depended on some uniformity in cataloging. The proposals of Florian Trefler (mid-sixteenth century), Gabriel Naudé, and John Dury (both seventeenth century) in their books on librarianship would have had some general application to cataloging in many libraries, but they were not sets of specific rules such as we expect in codes today. Booksellers' lists, notably that of Andrew Maunsell (1595), and bibliographies such as Konrad Gesner's (mid-sixteenth century) both recognized some uniformity of general practice and by their very existence promoted greater uniformity. Gesner, indeed, even suggested that a checked copy of his bibliography could serve as a catalog for an individual library. Only with Frederic Rostgaard's rather detailed suggestions (1698) and the much later instructions for cataloging the confiscated collections, issued by the French Revolutionary government (1791), do we have something like codes of general applications in the modern sense.

Cutter owed much to two of these individual codes: Panizzi's and Jewett's.

Sir Anthony Panizzi's famous ninety-one rules were adopted in 1839 as the basis for a new catalog of the British Museum, and they were published in an ill-fated first (and only) volume of that catalog in 1841. The ninety-one rules came at a time of long and earnest debate about the British Museum catalog involving famous librarians, scholarly users, and even a select committee of the House of Commons; and in the British Museum they were to last without major change for decades.

catalog of the Smithsonian Insti-
w cases from Panizzi's. Although
amphlet of thirty-three rules, he
be stringent and detailed: "Noth-
ld be left to the individual taste
shall find this attitude again.

themselves to the problems of lo-
author or its title, and they had
rticular scholarly research library,
ideas had universal implications.
dealt with the problems of locat-
as well as by its author and title;
n all kinds and sizes of libraries.
Cutter, "could be adopted in all
braries for study and the libraries
for reading have different objects . . . Without pretending to exactness, we may divide dictionary catalogs into short-title, medium-title,
and full-title or bibliographic; typical examples of the three being
1) The Boston Mercantile (1869) . . . 2) the Boston Public (1861
and 1866) . . . 3) the catalog now making by the Library of Congress . . . I shall use the three words Short, Medium, and Full as
proper names, with the preliminary caution that the Short family are
not all of the same size, that there is more than one Medium, and
that Full may be Fuller or Fullest" (p.11).

But Cutter wanted even more than a general code for all kinds of
entry for all kinds of libraries.

"There are plenty of treatises on classification," he wrote in the
prefatory note to the first edition, and "for an author-catalog there
are the famous 91 rules of the British Museum . . . Professor Jewett's modification of them . . . Mr. F. B. Perkins's further modification . . . and a chapter in the second volume of Edwards. But for a
dictionary catalog as a whole . . . there is no manual whatever. Nor
have any of the above-mentioned works attempted to set forth the
rules in a systematic way or to investigate what might be called the
first principles of cataloging. It is to be expected that a first attempt
will be incomplete, and I shall be obliged to librarians for criticisms,
objections, or new problems, with or without solutions. With such
assistance perhaps a second edition of these hints would deserve the
title—Rules."

"To set forth the rules in a systematic way" and "to investigate what might be called the first principles of cataloging," truly noble ambitions, in spite of the characteristically modest disclaimer.

Objects and Means

Cutter opened his rules with a statement of the objects and means of the catalog (p.12):

OBJECTS.

1. To enable a person to find a book of which either
   (A) the author ⎫
   (B) the title   ⎬ is known.
   (C) the subject ⎭
2. To show what the library has
   (D) by a given author
   (E) on a given subject
   (F) in a given kind of literature.
3. To assist in the choice of a book
   (G) as to its edition (bibliographically)
   (H) as to its character (literary or topical).

MEANS.

1. Author-entry with the necessary references (for A and D).
2. Title-entry or title-reference (for B).
3. Subject-entry, cross-references, and classed subject-table (for C and E).
4. Form-entry and language-entry (for F).
5. Giving edition and imprint, with notes when necessary (for G).
6. Notes (for H).

REASONS FOR CHOICE.

Among the several possible methods of attaining the OBJECTS, other things being equal, choose that entry
(1) That will probably be first looked under by the class of people who use the library;
(2) That is consistent with other entries, so that one principle can cover all;
(3) That will mass entries least in places where it is difficult to so arrange them that they can be readily found, as under names of nations and cities.
This applies very slightly to entries under first words, because it is easy and sufficient to arrange them by the alphabet.

In a footnote Cutter remarked that this statement "has been criticized; but it has also been frequently quoted, usually without change or credit, in the prefaces of catalogs and elsewhere. I suppose it has on the whole been approved." It has, indeed, been approved in American catalogs ever since, although still "usually without change or credit."

The Convenience of the Public

The statement of objects and means opened every edition of Cutter's *Rules*. A famous paragraph in the Preface to the fourth edition (p.6) stated a significant amendment:

> The convenience of the public is always to be set before the ease of the cataloger. In most cases they coincide. A plain rule without exceptions is not only easy for us to carry out, but easy for the public to understand and work by. But strict consistency in a rule and uniformity in its application sometimes lead to practices which clash with the public's habitual way of looking at things. When these habits are general and deeply rooted, it is unwise for the cataloger to ignore them, even if they demand a sacrifice of system and simplicity.

Offhand, this notion of the convenience of the public would seem to be in conflict with the idea of building a code about a statement of objects and means. It is true that the statement of objects and means is itself a statement of what is assumed (but not known) to be what the convenience of the public demands. But once Cutter had adopted his statement of objects and means, he had in fact adopted a bibliographical system. Could he allow the convenience of the public to interfere with the convenience of the bibliographical system?

Rules for a Printed Dictionary Catalogue

A statement of objects and means and a concession to the convenience of the public. On this foundation Cutter sought to "set forth the rules in a systematic way" and "to investigate what might be called the first principles of cataloging."

With each rule, whenever necessary, he told in detail the possible alternatives and the reasons why he had chosen as he did. Of course, a set of basic principles did not automatically bring few rules. "The number of the following rules," Cutter wrote, "is not owing to any complexity of system, but to the number of widely varying cases to which a few simple principles have to be applied" (p.11–12).

Books do, indeed, differ from one another in every way—and more—that you can dream of. The very best code of rules could not deal with *all* the possible variations. Even if we could think of all the possible variations, we should find that there is not often just one answer to the problem posed by each variation. Often there are two answers; sometimes there are many. Nor does the "convenience of the public" always help. Under whose name, for instance, would the user of a catalog expect to find John Doe's play based on Gustave Doe's novel? Under what subject would he expect to find Anastasia

Doe's penetrating study of the effect on catalogers of their social and economic status?

There is seldom just one "true" answer. But the cataloger must choose just one. And once he has chosen he must try to give the same answer to every other book with the same or similar problem. This is not pedantry. If one were to catalog today the same group of books he cataloged a month ago, he would do no more than two thirds of them in the same way he did them last month. (Cf. Ann Painter in *Library Resources and Technical Services*, 7:279–80 [1963].) If he were to catalog a group of books similar to (but not the same as) the group he cataloged a month ago, the difference in treatment would be much greater.

The size of Cutter's code grew with each new edition, and in the fourth and last (1904) we find him saying that "the increase in the number of rules is due chiefly not to making new rules, but to taking out from the long notes many recommendations that were in effect rules, and are more easily referred to and found in their present place. The changes are largely for the sake of greater clearness and of better classification" (p.6).

And always there was the problem of "convenience of the public" and how far the cataloger should adjust to it. "Cataloging is an art, not a science," he wrote at last. "No rules can take the place of experience and good judgment, but some of the results of experience may be best indicated by rules" (p.6).

The search for stability and order in the catalog and in the rules which produced it raised many questions. Can we have a few simple universal principles, or even with such principles would there be many rules? Should a code leave little to the cataloger's taste and judgment as Jewett demanded, or was Cutter right when he said that cataloging is an art demanding judgment? Do we need an individual code for each library; or a code to be used by all libraries everywhere? Do we need a code of strict logic; or a code based on "convenience of the public"? Or can we have both? Cutter asked many of the questions we still ask; he set them all out in orderly array, and in his thoughtful and thought-provoking classic he gave many of the answers we still give today.

2
The Prophet and the Law:
Codes after Cutter

The Anglo-American Code of 1908 (ALA 1908)

The year of Cutter's first edition (1876) was also the year of the birth of the American Library Association (ALA), and on September 5 of the very next year an ALA committee on cataloging was appointed. This committee submitted "Condensed Rules for an Author and Title Catalog" to the ALA Conference of 1883, and the rules were published in *Library Journal* and also in the third edition of Cutter's *Rules*.

Obviously it is wasteful for many catalogers all over the country each to catalog a copy of the same book. There was much talk of cooperative cataloging; yet cooperative cataloging is possible only if there is standardization. The climax came in an agreement between the ALA Publishing Board and LC by which the latter was to supply printed cards for current books beginning, if possible, January 1, 1901. ALA appointed a new Catalog Rules Committee to examine LC practices and recommend such changes as seemed necessary, and to consider the catalog rules in force, particularly those points on which American libraries had been unable to agree.

In order not to delay the issue of printed cards by LC, the Committee agreed that LC practice should be accepted tentatively. Further, the Committee wanted to get agreement between LC rules and the new ALA rules. In 1902 appeared a draft code, "A.L.A. Rules— Advance Edition," and in 1904 the Library Association (of the United Kingdom) proposed that it and ALA issue a joint code. The invitation was accepted and the Anglo-American code was published in 1908 in two editions (English and American) with notes explaining the relatively few points on which there was a difference of opinion.

The new code owed much to Cutter; he was one of the most active members of the Committee till his death, September 3, 1903. But there were differences. The statement of "Objects" and "Means" disappeared, although Cutter's famous paragraph about "the convenience of the public" was quoted in full (p.ix). Here it served to strengthen the Committee's contention that although the alternatives and exceptions and variations in the rules for societies and institutions might be "open to the charge of inconsistency," the rules nonetheless would bring "the vast majority" of these bodies "under the heading where they are most likely to be looked for." There were no rules for subject headings: "A new edition of the List of Subject Headings will to some extent deal with these questions" (p.x). Finally, the new code was a set of rules without reasons; gone were the illuminating discussions which so often accompanied individual rules in Cutter's code. It took into consideration the practices of LC. Instructions to the Committee in 1901 called for "a code of rules which should be in accord with the system governing the compilation of catalog entries at the Library of Congress . . . The Committee found that under the circumstances its decisions must be guided chiefly by the requirements of larger libraries of a scholarly character; that only incidentally would it be possible to outline modifications or variations of practice suitable for the smaller libraries. Later it was decided that a simplified edition . . . would prove more effective than occasional directions and variations . . ." (p.viii).

ALA 1908 was thus broader than Cutter's *Rules* in that it represented the international agreement of two national library associations, and the sanction of those associations would perhaps win greater uniformity than a single individual even of Cutter's stature could hope for. At the same time, the new code was narrower than Cutter's: It was drawn up for large research libraries only, and it was in harmony with LC practice. It had no rules for subject headings; for the future, subject headings would conform not to a code but to a record of decisions, the list of subject headings. Finally, it was content with only the first of Cutter's ambitions: "To set forth the rules in a systematic way." Missing was the second: "To investigate what might be called the first principles of cataloging." Perhaps it seemed that these were now obvious.

The single author had yielded to the committee; the prophet had given way to the law. Yet does either the prophet's dream or the law's detail matter so much as what is actually *done*? In the future could even the best code in the world mean much if LC cards did not follow it?

"On seeing the great success of the Library of Congress cataloging," Cutter had begun the Preface to his fourth and last edition, "I doubted whether it was worth while to issue this fourth edition of my Rules . . . I cannot help thinking that the golden age of cataloging is over, and that the difficulties and discussions which have furnished an innocent pleasure to so many will interest them no more. Another lost art."

Prussian Instructions (PI)

In 1908 also was published *The Prussian Instructions* (PI). Like ALA 1908, these instructions had been developing over many years and owed much to the original thinking of individual librarians, particularly Dziatzko and Milkau. As ALA 1908 influenced the library practice of English-speaking peoples, so PI was to have a profound influence on Germanic peoples. It differed from ALA 1908 in at least two important respects: (1) It preferred entry under title instead of corporate entry, and (2) it preferred grammatical arrangement of title entries instead of natural (or mechanical, as it is sometimes called) arrangement. The American Catalog Rules Committee had "watched with great interest" German developments, and, although it felt there was "little likelihood of agreement on the two fundamental points of difference," the Committee had nonetheless sought "in formulating our own decisions to bear in mind the possibility of future international agreement and cooperation" (p.x).

For fifty years the Western cataloging world was divided between the philosophies of these two codes, ALA 1908 and PI.

ALA Draft, 1941 (ALA 1941)

ALA 1908 had been a pamphlet of 88 pages; in 1941 a "Preliminary American Second Edition" appeared with 408 pages (ALA 1941). Cutter's rules had multiplied also in their day, but, as he had pointed out, they all grew out of his brief statement of simple principles; the additions were only lifted from the commentary of earlier editions for ease of reference. The reason for the expansion in 1941 was different.

The 1941 preface noted that since 1908 there had been "steady progress in the standardization of library catalogs furthered by the increasing use of Library of Congress printed cards" (p.vii). Individual libraries had followed LC practice even for the cards they produced themselves, so that their catalogs would be consistent. Co-operative cataloging had increased; scholarly libraries over the country were contributing copy to LC.

The way to keep the record had been found; all catalogers needed to do now was to keep to the way. Elaborate and precise detail, this was the way. The job would never have to be done over again; they were cataloging for eternity. All this left, as Jewett had once urged, little room for "individual taste or judgment of the cataloger." Cutter, on the other hand, had felt that "cataloging is an art, not a science." Cataloging was no longer an art, nor was it a science; it was an elaborate technique whose sole aim was standardization.

But, meanwhile, there had been no revision of ALA 1908, apart from the supplementary rules on cards and two pamphlets on periodicals and corporate body serial publications issued by LC. The Preface complained that catalogers lost much time seeking rules or trying to deduce LC practice from study of LC cards or even writing to LC. "Dissatisfaction with the 1908 code rested not with its inclusions but rather with its omissions . . . Expansion was needed rather than change" (p.viii). The subcommittee originally appointed by the ALA Committee on Cataloging and Classification became in 1932 an independent ALA committee "to make necessary revisions in the A.L.A. Catalog rules with authority to cooperate with the Library Association of Great Britain and with such other national library associations as it may think appropriate." A Carnegie Corporation grant in 1936 brought help to the Committee, hitherto dependent on voluntary efforts.

As that of 1908, the draft of 1941 omitted subject headings. Although the Committee "was well aware that small libraries had no urgent need of so detailed a code," it was suggested merely that the question of a separate simplified code "should be considered further after this one has had a period of trial" (p.xiii). Unlike ALA 1908, the draft was divided into two parts, one dealing with "entry and heading," the other with "actual description of the book" (p.xii). More important, the Second World War had brought an abrupt close to the plans for international cooperation.

Osborn's "Crisis"

ALA 1941 was the product of over a decade's devoted work by many able people, and it gave all the detailed instructions which catalogers insisted they needed. The law had put the final touch to the prophet.

Triumph was short-lived. On June 21, 1941, Andrew D. Osborn attacked the draft in his famous "The Crisis in Cataloging." The paper's title was dramatic, the style was popular, and in its sweeping generalizations the simmering frustrations of a generation of library administrators came to boil. Everybody read it, everybody talked about it, many wrote about it. The paper gave a name and an atmosphere to an era which has not yet closed.

Most of all, Osborn denounced what he called "legalistic" cataloging. Cataloging, he insisted, is an art (shades of Cutter!) and it needs only a few basic rules. But the "legalist" demands a rule for every question that has ever come up or may come up. There are, he felt, at least three defects in the legalistic approach: (1) Rules try to cover matters of taste and judgment which must be left indefinite. (Jewett had thought otherwise of taste and judgment; see p.5 above.) (2) The costly business of debate and rule-making goes on forever. (3) "Codification tends to obscure reasons and principles . . . Elements of cataloging practice that were introduced for historical reasons come to be perpetuated without any understanding of why the rule was made."

The prophet had returned. But it was a return with a strange ally. "The foremost problem confronting library administrators," wrote Osborn, was "the cost of cataloging." Behind the prophet who wanted simplification because it would save basic principles stood the library administrator who wanted simplification because he thought it would save money. An uneasy alliance.

LC Studies of Descriptive Cataloging

LC's *Studies of Descriptive Cataloging* appeared in 1946. It contained a statement of basic principles not unlike those which had been in Cutter's "Objects," and it suggested that these principles could be served adequately by brief and simple description. Proof lay in Elizabeth G. Pierce's study of the value of full title-page transcription as a means of identifying the book; she found that brief description would identify books equally well. Also included was Seymour Lubetzky's devastating theoretical analysis of current detailed practice in descriptive cataloging. Practicing catalogers were brought in also with a conference at LC and with a questionnaire sent out with the statement of principles and examples. In general, they strongly approved the proposed simplification.

Interlude: The Vatican Code of 1948

Irony dogged the Vatican Code on the American scene from the first. In the late 1920's the Carnegie Endowment for International Peace offered to help establish a new and completely uniform catalog of the Vatican Library. Several of the Library's staff members were trained in American library schools, and there was an American mission to Rome which included James C. M. Hanson and Charles Martel, architects of the then developing LC cataloging practice. The detailed Vatican Code prepared at that time drew heavily on this practice, and, like Cutter's *Rules,* it also included rules for subject headings. Thus it came about that for many years the best and most complete statement of American cataloging practice was in Italian.

As noted above, this was a time when LC was leading American cataloging down a twisting path which catalogers found ever more hard to follow—or even to find. There were repeated proposals for an English translation of the Italian guide. Finally, in 1940 the translation was completed, and then World War II prevented publication until 1948. But by 1948 the elaborate ALA 1941 had long since swept aside the urgent need for such a guide as the Vatican Code; catalogers had wrangled for six years over the details of ALA 1941; and it was the eve of publication of the ALA-LC codes of 1949. The Vatican Code in English had slight impact on American cataloging; it remains only an intriguing historical curiosity.

ALA-LC Codes, 1949 (ALA 1949 and LC 1949)

After the LC *Studies* of 1946, LC started work on its own rules for description. A preliminary edition in 1947 was followed in 1949 by a final edition (LC 1949), which ALA adopted as a substitute for Part II of the 1941 draft.

Meanwhile, the ALA special committee had found Part I of the 1941 draft (author and title entry) acceptable both to LC and to other research libraries, and the committee urged that a final edition of this part be prepared. These rules were issued by the ALA, also in 1949 (ALA 1949).

The 1949 rules are a curious pair of books. They carried one step further that divisive specialization begun when ALA 1908 abandoned subject headings and non-research libraries; now, in 1949 we had a volume on entry and a volume on description. Missing also was the British cooperation of 1908, although the ALA 1949 preface tells us that the British committee had "been kept informed of progress and general agreement is assured" (p.x).

The ALA 1949 preface drew largely from the preface of ALA 1941, including the statement about dissatisfaction with omissions rather than inclusions in the 1908 code. Chief changes from 1941 were in rearrangement of the material "to make the sequence . . . logical so far as possible" (p.ix) and in reduction of the number of alternate rules. The Introduction stated that the rules were "intended to represent the best or the most general current practice . . . They are not few nor are they . . . simple, for the material to which they are to be applied is almost as multitudinous and complicated as humanity itself" (p.xix). They were intended to "aid the cataloger in the choice of entry and form of heading so that a reasonable degree of standardization . . . may prevail" not only in individual catalogs but also in centralized and cooperative cataloging, union catalogs, and bibliographies (p.xix). There followed some few general principles not unlike those in Cutter's "Objects," although Cutter was specifically mentioned only with an approving nod toward his famous "convenience of the public" paragraph.

LC 1949, on the other hand, broke completely with the 1941 draft. It opened with a statement of "Principles of Descriptive Cataloging" derived from the LC *Studies* of 1946. It stated that these principles "provide a common basis for the rules" and that they would, therefore, make it possible for the cataloger "faced with problems not specifically provided for, to solve them in the spirit and intent of the rules given below" (p.7). The Foreword and Introduction breathe a new liberalism. They admit, for instance, that special needs in the LC catalog have been "often a deciding factor in the adoption of certain rules" and suggest that other libraries "will have to decide for themselves at what point they wish to depart" from these. The uniformity secured by "a single set of rules" is necessary for "cooperative cataloging and international bibliography"; but "cataloging for purely local uses need not conform if local needs do not require conformity" (p.vi). And there is recognition of future change: "While the basic principles of a cataloging system should not fluctuate from year to year changes in detail can be made . . . whenever improvements are discovered" (p.5). This last was, perhaps, most important, for the rules in LC 1949 did not carry simplifications and brevity in cataloging nearly as far as the general principles might have allowed.

So ALA 1949 had stuck to what was being done; LC 1949 had returned to Cutter's goal: "to investigate what might be called the first principles of cataloging."

Seymour Lubetzky

Critics of the codes of 1949 found fault with the detail of ALA 1949 and praised the LC 1949 search for principles. Cataloging practice at LC and elsewhere confirmed the critics. A supplement to the LC rules in 1952 and an ALA-LC list of additions and changes published in 1959 sharply cut the detail provided in both codes.

In 1953, Seymour Lubetzky's *Cataloging Rules and Principles*, a thorough study of the ALA code, appeared. Lubetzky, a member of the staff of LC, had been assigned by it to make the study for the Board on Cataloging Policy and Research of the ALA Division of Cataloging and Classification. First he dealt with the structure of the code: "Is this rule necessary?" Time and again his relentless logic showed that it was not a necessary rule and that it was not properly related to any other rule. Each rule dealt with some specific question rather than with the general situation which the problem represented. His approach to corporate entry was historical as well as logical. The conclusion was equally damning: The historical reason for distinguishing between kinds of corporate bodies had been forgotten in the fascinating business of building the distinctions. (This was precisely what Osborn had said would happen.) In a final chapter on the design of a code, Lubetzky put forward two "objectives" (see p.27–28 below), similar to the two "Objects" for entry and heading which Cutter suggested in 1876 (see p.6 above); and he showed in rough outline how a code built on them (without Cutter's emphasis on "convenience of the public") might look.

Reaction to the Lubetzky Report was generally favorable. Another Catalog Code Revision Committee was appointed. Wyllis Wright was chairman and in 1956, Seymour Lubetzky was appointed editor. Editor and Committee were responsible to the Division of Cataloging and Classification (later the Cataloging and Classification Section of the Resources and Technical Services Division) of ALA.

Procedure for code revision was simple. First drafts of rules or blocks of rules were drawn up by Lubetzky. They were then submitted for discussion to the section heads and specialists of the LC Descriptive Cataloging Division, the Steering Committee of the Code Revision Committee, and finally to the full Committee itself, some thirty people drawn from all kinds of libraries. In addition, at two week-long institutes—Stanford University in 1958 and McGill University in 1960—the Editor and Committee submitted their work to all who wished to attend (some two hundred at each institute) and share in the discussion.

In preparation for the McGill Institute of 1960, ALA printed the Lubetzky draft of the code as far as it had gone. The Lubetzky draft of 1960 (Lubetzky 1960) begins with the statement of the two objectives and then moves on to rules which in general rest logically upon them. Occasionally, however, Lubetzky found it necessary to depart from a logical interpretation of the objectives; we shall deal with some of these departures in the next chapter. In any event, these departures marked tacit acceptance of Cutter's "convenience of the public." Yet the two objectives themselves state no more than presumed "convenience of the public"; the fault with "convenience of the public" arises when it is allowed constantly to interfere with the operation of general principles in special cases. "Convenience" may properly interfere with logic only when urgent practical considerations are involved. The draft was accompanied by a commentary which tried to explain the reasoning behind the rules.

Like ALA 1908, Lubetzky 1960 represented the cooperation of British and American catalogers, and it was hoped that the completed code would serve all English-speaking peoples.

The Paris Statement: October 1961 (Paris 1961)

In 1954 the Council of the International Federation of Library Associations (IFLA) had set up an international working group to study the international coordination of cataloging rules; and Unesco encouraged and assisted IFLA's work in this field. Two grants from the Council on Library Resources enabled IFLA to plan and hold an International Conference on Cataloging Principles in Paris, October 9–18, 1961. Delegations from fifty-three countries and twelve international organizations attended. Working papers and a draft statement of principles were circulated before the Conference, and the sessions of the Conference were devoted to discussion and amendment of the draft. The final statement received the approval of a large majority of the participants.

The Paris Statement leans heavily on Lubetzky 1960. It begins with a statement of two functions quite similar to the two objectives of Cutter and Lubetzky. The principles themselves grow logically out of these two statements of function and generally agree with the Lubetzky rules. Perhaps the most dramatic thing about Paris 1961 is that it marked agreement of the Anglo-American and the *Prussian Instructions* schools of cataloging. Paris 1961 endorsed corporate entry and natural (or mechanical), rather than grammatical, arrangement of titles.

Although Paris 1961 professes to deal with principles rather than with rules, the principles are often so detailed as almost to be rules. The principles apply only to "choice and form of headings and entry words . . . in catalogs of printed books." Like the American codes after Cutter, they applied primarily to the catalogs of "large general libraries," although they were recommended "with such modifications as may be required" for other library catalogs and "other alphabetical lists of books."

Anglo-American Code, 1967 (ALA 1967): Compromise

When the Catalog Code Revision Committee was first appointed, it was proposed that the new code would be worked out without regard to the cost of change in existing catalogs. The first thing to do was to get a good code. Actually it never did work out quite that way. Discussion in Committee meetings and at the Stanford and

McGill institutes showed from the first a real concern for cost of change, and the rules of Lubetzky 1960 departed now and again from logic to meet what seemed to be a practical need.

After publication of Lubetzky 1960, cost came to be the major consideration. It was to be a code for research libraries, yet the Association of Research Libraries, led by the biggest research library of all, LC, insisted that it would be too costly to change their existing card catalogs to conform to the code. The form of the catalog (a file of cards) and the ideal of standardization (called up by widespread distribution of LC cards) thus became chains around the prophet's feet. The alliance between the prophet and the library administrator, begun with Osborn's "Crisis," always uneasy, came to an end.

The Catalog Code Revision Committee agreed to work out a code which would suit ARL and LC on those points that they insisted would cost too much to change (chiefly in the treatment of corporate entry). Thus, ironically, American catalogers whose pioneer work had inspired Paris 1961 were themselves unable to carry out a crucial part of it in their own code.

Meanwhile, Seymour Lubetzky had joined the faculty of the University of California at Los Angeles and found little time free to continue as editor. He resigned in 1962 and was succeeded by Sumner Spalding, also of the LC staff. The Council on Library Resources supplied the funds necessary for completion of the work.

ALA 1967: Conclusion

Under Sumner Spalding work on the code moved ahead much as it had under Seymour Lubetzky. The Editor submitted drafts to the section heads of the LC Descriptive Cataloging Division, to the Steering Committee of the ALA Catalog Code Revision Committee, and, finally, to the full Committee itself. There were two major differences: (1) the new LC representative on the Steering Committee, Lucile Morsch, had authority to speak for the Library, and (2) Paris 1961 (rather than the Lubetzky Report or the two objectives or Lubetzky 1960) was the base on which the code rested. Cooperation with the Library Association continued both by correspondence and by visits.

As work with entry got well under way again, the ALA Cataloging and Classification Section's Descriptive Cataloging Committee and the LC Descriptive Cataloging Division began to revise LC 1949; thus rules for description could again (as in 1908) be published with rules for entry. Bernice Field was chairman of the ALA committee, and Lucile Morsch represented LC and served as editor. Representatives of the Library Association worked with the Americans for awhile, but the rules for description in LA 1967 depart somewhat more from

LC 1949 than do those in ALA 1967 (see ALA 1967, p.371, and LA 1967, p.vi).

Also included in the code were the LC rules for cataloging "special" (or non-book) material.

ALA 1967 was a compromise and, like many compromises, it was not an inspiring document. To catalogers who had worked on the code (or even simply thought and debated about it) during the excitement of the Lubetzky years when a revolution seemed in the making, it was a disappointment. The new code was not a dramatic statement of what might be; instead, time and again, it seemed only to state current practice.

Yet, in a way, ALA 1967 was a massive achievement. It did, in a number of areas, move ahead of the 1949 codes and follow Paris 1961. It did, in most cases, manage to organize its (often quite detailed and specific) rules about definitely stated principles. It did, at last, bring into one document rules for entry and description for both book and non-book material. It did, to some extent (to a major extent with author and title entry), again represent British and American cooperation. (See ALA 1967, p.371, and LA 1967, p.v–vii and p.297–303.)

It was, no doubt, the most expensive code ever written. Many thousands of dollars from LC, ALA, and the Council on Library Resources were spent, and hundreds (perhaps many hundreds) of thousands of hours of work by many devoted people. Even at the legal minimum wage this would mean quite an investment.

ALA 1967 may be the last major code ever written for card catalogs. The card catalogs of LC and the large research libraries demanded its basic compromise. But even as the code was being written, LC and these same major research libraries were pushing ahead with plans for automation; and the book catalog business was booming. Finally, along with ALA 1967 came the LC decision on "superimposition": LC would apply the new rules only to works new to its collection and to headings for persons and corporate bodies being established for the first time; there would, of course, be a few exceptions. Thus, although LC had played a major part in code revision, its cards would not always conform to the results of that revision.

The COSATI Standard

In December 1963 the Committee on Scientific and Technical Information of the Federal Council for Science and Technology issued *Standard for Descriptive Cataloging of Government Scientific and Technical Reports*, designed primarily to achieve uniform cataloging by government agencies of such reports. The *Standard* (much briefer than other codes) differed in several ways from ALA 1967 then in preparation. For instance, it preferred main entry under a corporate body rather than under a personal author, and its heading for the added entry for a personal author tended to be briefer than the ALA 1967 heading for a personal name. The *Standard* consciously tried to provide rules which could be followed by relatively untrained people, and it sought to make it possible for the various agencies to exchange announcement and index copy and even machine tapes with intellectual content compatible. Thus a report would have to be cataloged only once.

The *Standard* had been prepared independently of the ALA Catalog Code Revision Committee. After its publication some attempt was made to reconcile the approaches but with little success. Revised versions of the *Standard* come somewhat closer to the practice of ALA 1967.

Because most general libraries which collect technical reports rely on the indexing and abstracting journals for control of such material, and because the number of individual reports cataloged like other material in general libraries is probably quite low, the *Standard* has not been considered in detail in Chapter 3 on author and title entry and heading.

Subject Headings and Classification

Cutter provided the first and the last American code for subject headings in his *Rules*. With ALA 1908 catalogers were referred to "The List of Subject Headings now in preparation" (p.x), and there the matter has stood ever since. There have been other lists, notably those of Sears and LC, but they have been only lists of terms catalogers were using. The Vatican Code, translated into English in 1948 (see p.13 above), like Cutter, had a section on subject headings, but it was largely a restatement of Cutter. Also, the Introductions to the various editions of the Sears list have had rules of a sort, again derived largely from Cutter. Cutter's successors who have dealt with the problem as a whole, Julia Pettee and David Haykin, did not follow Cutter in the attempt "to investigate what might be called the first principles of cataloging"; they sought only to arrange inherited practice into some sort of system.

For library classification there has been only one general code, that of William Stetson Merrill. A mimeographed version appeared in 1914, and the first printed edition, with rules revised and rearranged, in 1928. The second edition of the *Code for Classifiers*, issued in 1939, was much expanded, largely on the basis of thirty replies to one hundred copies of a circular letter sent out by ALA Publishing Department to librarians, library school teachers, and classifiers.

The *Code* begins with a statement of six "general principles," and then gives rules for various classes or forms of material. The bulk of the book is taken up with "classification under special subjects." In spite of the opening statement of principles, the sometimes rather detailed rules derive primarily from what was actually being done in libraries of whose practice Merrill had any knowledge. There has been no edition since 1939.

The *Guide to the Use of Dewey Decimal Classification* (1962) is a manual based, as the title page states, "on the practice of the Decimal Classification Office of the Library of Congress." It is, thus, simply a record of decisions, comparable to the various subject heading lists; and much of it was absorbed in the text of the seventeenth edition of Dewey.

Broadly speaking, the better the code the less need there is for a record of decisions. The code lays out the ground rules; the record tells only what has been done when the rules were not clear enough or specific enough. If the rules lack a basic philosophy or are too few in number, there is more need for the record. The codes for author and title entry and description have been more fully developed than codes for subject headings and classification. In consequence, the lists have flourished in these two areas.

The Prophet and the Law

The story of cataloging codes in America is the story of the prophet and the law. The dreams of the prophet have lasting value only if they are set down in writing. Here there is conflict: How much should be set down?

The prophet is content to say: "Love God, love your neighbor." This is simple enough. It should be easy to apply and it should cover all of life. The prophet will say that to apply the rule wisely is not always to apply it consistently because of the infinite variety in the conditions of life. He will say that to apply the rule well is better than to apply it consistently. He will say that to apply the rule is an art.

But the law sets down much. The law tells you what love is and what God is and precisely how to love Him and when; and the law tells you which neighbor is meant and how to love him and when. The law will say that to apply the rule wisely is always to apply it consistently because of the infinite variety in the conditions of life. The law will say that to apply the rule consistently is to apply the rule well. The law will say that to apply the rule is a technique.

But the prophet and the law have to reckon with practice. The prophet's dream and the law's detail mean little if people *do* something else. In nineteenth-century cataloging the prophets and the law and practice all changed from time to time and from place to place. In the twentieth century LC printed cards froze practice. Twentieth-century codes at first tried only to discover LC practice and to reconcile it with that of other libraries. But LC is a large research library; to fashion a code by its practice meant to squeeze out the non-research libraries which Cutter had served along with their giant brethren. Also it meant standardization, with an eye ever on the union catalog and cooperative cataloging rather than concern for the special needs of individual libraries.

Practice is powerful because of the innate conservatism of man; whatever is, is right. Practice is powerful also because of the cost of change. A file of catalog cards built up over a period of fifty years or more is a major investment. The prophet's dream or the law's detail may be better than what is in that file, but they would cost money. The twentieth-century prophet was welcome only so long as it seemed that the simplification he dreamed of would save cataloging time, i.e., money.

In general, the codes after Cutter sought to turn the work of the prophet into law—rather detailed law designed for a large, scholarly library. We shall now examine some of the specific effects of this effort.

3

Who Did It?
Author and Title Entry and Heading

"Entry," wrote Cutter in 1876, is "the registry of a book in the catalogue . . ." In ALA 1967 (p.344) "Entry" is "a record of a bibliographical entity in a catalog or list . . ." But "registry" or "record" *where* in the catalog?

If the user wants a book by Thomas Mann, probably he will look in the catalog under "Mann, Thomas." But why? After all, every book has a name. Its name is a title. The title would seem to be the first way to identify the book, just as a man's name is the first way to identify the man. The author of a book is secondary; we may not even remember the author's name. Why arrange books by authors' names?

Early lists of books (such as those of Sumer, ca. 2000 B.C.) and later lists continuing through the Middle Ages (such as the list of Glastonbury Abbey) generally have at least three things in common: (1) They show only a rough idea, if any, that sequence of entries matters. (2) They deal with only a few books (Sumer, 62; Glastonbury, 340). (3) Possibly few were "catalogs" in the modern sense of the word; the Sumer list may have been a sort of "bibliography" and the Glastonbury list a sort of "inventory."

The idea of entry under author may be associated with the growth of large collections and the need to arrange long lists of books in some way. Fragments of the list compiled by Callimachus of Alexandria about 250 B.C. (probably a bibliography of Greek literature rather than a catalog of the Alexandrian library), as well as fragments of other Greek bibliographies, suggest arrangement under broad subject and under each subject by author. Apparently entry under author is part of our Greek inheritance; in the Orient entry is traditionally under title.

There is also some logic in entry under author. Although the author is, perhaps, a secondary means of identifying a book, ordinarily the user will know both author and title, and if entry is under author instead of under title, all the works of an author will come together.

The printing press brought mass production of books. Problems of arrangement were much more urgent. Again the bibliographers led the catalogers. Toward the end of the fifteenth century Tritheim added an alphabetical author index to his chronologically arranged bibliography. Konrad Gesner's author bibliography of 1545 followed current custom in using the forename first. In a catalog of 1595, Maunsell, a bookseller, finally made entries under surnames rather than forenames. Entry under forename, however, survived in many library catalogs for many years. Thus only gradually, at the end of many centuries, did we come to "Mann, Thomas."

What Is an Author?

What is an author? The answer is obvious: He wrote the book. Did he now? Who wrote the works of Gilbert and Sullivan? Who wrote Pope's Homer? Who wrote the annual report of the John Doe Society? Who wrote Josiah Doe's anthology of poems on catalogers? Sometimes the answer is obvious; sometimes it is not.

Only if we have a rather definite idea of what we mean by "author" shall we know how to enter a book in our catalog. What is an author? Perhaps no other question is more important to the cataloger.

We begin with Cutter: "*Author,* in the narrower sense, is the person who writes a book; in a wider sense it may be applied to him who is the cause of the book's existence by putting together the writings of several authors (usually called *the editor,* more properly to be called *the collector*). Bodies of men (societies, cities, legislative bodies, countries) are to be considered the authors of their memoirs, transactions, journals, debates, reports, etc." (p.14).

ALA 1908: "1. The writer of a book, as distinguished from translator, editor, etc. 2. In a broader sense, the maker of the book or the person or body immediately responsible for its existence. Thus, a person who collects and puts together the writings of several authors (compiler or editor) may be said to be the author of a collection. Corporate bodies may be considered the authors of publications issued in their name or by their authority" (p.xiii).

ALA 1941 differs only in that for some reason it speaks of "a corporate body" instead of "corporate bodies" and at this point refers the reader to rules for corporate bodies (p.xv–xvi).

ALA 1949 revises the first part of the definition to read: "The writer of a work, as distinguished from the translator, editor, etc. By extension, an artist, composer, photographer, cartographer, etc." In the second part the word "book" is replaced by "work." Otherwise the definition reads as in ALA 1941.

The definitions noted above all appear in lists of definitions published with the respective codes. Under Rule 1, however, ALA 1949 expands its definition: "The author is considered to be the person or body chiefly responsible for the intellectual content of the book, literary, artistic or musical . . . Governments, societies, institutions, and other organizations are to be regarded as authors of the publications for which they as corporate bodies are responsible, but the papers, addresses, etc., of their officials, members or employees as individuals, are entered under personal author, even though issued by the corporate body" (p.3).

There is no definition of "author" in Lubetzky 1960 or in Paris 1961. ALA 1967: "By author is meant the person or corporate body chiefly responsible for the creation of the intellectual or artistic content of a work. Thus composers, artists, photographers, etc., are the 'authors' of the works they create; chess players are the 'authors' of their recorded games; etc. The term 'author' also embraces an editor or compiler who has primary responsibility for the content of a work, e.g., the compiler of a bibliography" (Chap. 1, p.9, footnote 2; the Glossary, p.343, has a somewhat abbreviated version). This definition seems to raise at least two questions: (1) Are baseball players, like chess players, the " 'authors' of their recorded games"? If so, what of the sportswriter who records their games? (2) Is "compiler of a bibliography" an appropriate example? Surely there is no doubt that such a compiler is the responsible author of his work. Perhaps what is intended is such a person as a compiler of a collection of poems by various authors.

What is an author? The answer is clear enough when we have only one person writing a book. The answer becomes less clear as more people and more kinds of books enter the picture. So the definitions of "author" all begin with one person and the conventional written book. Then each seeks to broaden the definition, to get under the tent of authorship books written by more than one person and books other than the conventional written book.

The device used is the concept of responsibility. Cutter's phrase "the cause of the book's existence" applies only to a personal author, and he arbitrarily adds that corporate bodies "are to be considered" authors. ALA 1908 sharpens the definition: The author is the "person or body immediately responsible" for the book's existence. Finally, ALA 1949 uses the broader term "work" and states that an author may be a "writer" but also may be "an artist, composer, photographer, cartographer, etc." ALA 1949 is even more specific: "the person or body chiefly responsible for the intellectual content of the book, literary, artistic, or musical." ALA 1967 is equally broad.

The idea that corporate bodies may be authors is a logical extension of the modern notion that the corporate body is a corporate person entitled, like any other person, to buy property and to sell it, to make money and to lose it, to obey the law and to violate it. The private person may do all these things and many other things as long as he is responsible for what he does. So it is with the corporate body: Responsibility comes with the right to act. Just as the private person is responsible for the intellectual content of the book of which he is an author, so the corporate body is responsible for the intellectual content of the book of which it is an author.

Is this extension of the definition of "author" justified? Probably. Entry under author is only a matter of convention in Western civilization. That the convention took many centuries to gain favor does not make it sacred or unique. It is useful in determining entry only because it *is* a convention and therefore gives us a design of entry easily explained and understood; that is, it meets Cutter's criterion of "convenience of the public." But conventions constantly change; the cataloger is free to make his contribution to that change.

At the same time, the cataloger's addition to convention must be as easily explained and understood as the original convention; otherwise it will not serve the "convenience of the public." Thus, it is easy to understand that the John Doe Society is "responsible" for the intellectual content of its annual report; but will it serve the "convenience of the public" to consider the John Doe Society the author of books which it publishes but for whose content the Society assumes no responsibility? Who is "responsible" or even (to use the additional qualification of ALA 1949 and ALA 1967) "chiefly responsible" for the works of Gilbert and Sullivan or for Pope's Homer? Is a map more usefully entered under the "author" who is "responsible"—i.e., the cartographer—or under the place represented on the map? Josiah Doe is "responsible" for the intellectual content he chooses to put into his anthology; therefore, he is the "author." Yet the idea of the compiler as author—accepted in definition since Cutter—is hedged with exceptions in Cutter (98–108), ALA 1908 (126), and ALA 1949 (5A); and it is permitted in Lubetzky 1960 (4), Paris 1961 (10.34), and ALA 1967 (4–5) only if the compiler is named on the title page.

Entry under author is by no means a cure-all, even with the greatly expanded definition of "author." Indeed, entry under author serves sharply and clearly only for the conventional book with a single responsible author, personal or corporate.

Heading

The heading is the word or phrase which heads an entry: it indicates some special aspect of the book such as authorship or subject. Because entries in a dictionary catalog are arranged alphabetically, choice of heading will make an entry easy (or hard) for the user of the catalog to find. The heading for a book will, of course, be the author's name, inverted to bring the surname first if the author is a person.

How much of the name? "Tarkington, Booth" or "Tarkington, Newton Booth"? "Still Research Institute" or "A. T. Still Research Institute"? Is anything to be added to the name? "Shakespeare, William" or "Shakespeare, William, 1564–1616"? "Roosevelt, Franklin Delano" or "Roosevelt, Franklin Delano, President"? "The Club" or "The Club, Rochester, N.Y."?

And which name? "Twain, Mark" or "Clemens, Samuel Langhorne"? "Charlotte Brontë" under "Brontë" or under her married name "Nicholls"? "Ratti, Achille" or "Pius XI, Pope"? "Pennsylvania State College" or "Pennsylvania State University"? "Unesco" or "United Nations Educational, Scientific, and Cultural Organization"?

The list could go on forever. Petty, pedantic puttering it seems, all of it. Yet in every case the exact place in the catalog where the user must look to find an entry is affected. Codes seek to bring as many of these little questions as possible under general rules which have a reasonable basis; this approach best serves the "convenience of the public" because it means the rules can be easily explained and readily understood. At some point, however, logic and general rules fail; there is nothing left but to be arbitrary.

The Two Objectives

Cutter's "Objects" (see p.6 above) first tried to give a broad and definite answer, to bring the problems into focus. So far as author entry is concerned, he suggested that the objects of the catalog are two:

1. To enable a person to find a book of which the author or the title is known, and
2. To show what the library has by a given author.

Although these two objectives are implied in the various ALA Codes, they were not again specifically stated as the groundwork of a code until Lubetzky 1960 (p.ix):

> The objectives which the catalog is to serve are two:
>
> First, to facilitate the location of a particular publication, i.e., of a particular edition of a work which is in the library.

Second, to relate and display together the editions which a library has of a given work and the works which it has of a given author.

Paris 1961 again rephrased them as "functions of the catalogue" (2):

The catalogue should be an efficient instrument for ascertaining
2.1 whether the library contains a particular book specified by
    (a) its author and title, or
    (b) if the author is not named in the book, its title alone, or
    (c) if author and title are inappropriate or insufficient for identi-
        fication, a suitable substitute for the title; and
2.2 (a) which works by a particular author and
    (b) which editions of a particular work are in the library.

Apart from their content, at least three aspects of these two objectives need to be remembered:

1. They are not new; they are as old as Cutter's first edition (1876) and they have been in our American codes (implied or stated in so many words) ever since.

2. They may conflict with Cutter's concern about "convenience of the public," but they simply state what the code writer thinks the "convenience of the public" demands first of all (see p.7 above).

3. They will be most efficiently served by headings as brief as possible. Each entry need be only as full as is necessary to set it apart and thus make it easy to find. Brevity is, however, not peculiar to cataloging. It is common sense in all kinds of communication.

Author Headings

What does all this mean in the search for a heading of the entry for a conventional book with a single responsible author? The first objective looks at a book as an individual; the second objective looks at the book as one of a group of books. Cutter recognized an inherent conflict (p.31):

> It must be remembered that the object is not merely to facilitate the finding of a given book by an author's name. If this were all, it might have been better to make the entry, as proposed by Mr. Crestadoro, under the part of the name mentioned in the title, which would lead to having *Bulwer* in one book, *Lytton* in another, *Bulwer-Lytton* in a third . . . This might have been best with [the first objective] . . . but we have also [the second objective] . . . to provide for—the finding of all the books of a given author—and this can most conveniently be done if they are all collected in one place.

Thus Cutter resolved the conflict by making the second objective more important than the first: For each author there would be a uniform heading. Code writers since Cutter have followed his lead.

But authors' names may change. Which form of the author's name do we choose for the uniform heading? We may take one of two basic approaches. Neither approach is logical; both approaches are arbitrary.

First, we may be rigid.

We then choose the author's "real" name. If we do this, we have "Clemens, Samuel Langhorne," not "Twain, Mark"; "Tarkington, Newton Booth," not "Tarkington, Booth"; "United Nations Educational, Scientific, and Cultural Organization," not "Unesco." Generally, this was the choice of the ALA codes until 1967. Broadly speaking, it requires more work of the cataloger and a rather comprehensive reference collection; not all names are as obvious as Clemens. Such a reference collection is, however, to be found in the large research libraries for which these codes were written.

If the author's "real" name changes, we choose the latest form of the name. This means "Nicholls, Charlotte (Brontë)," not "Brontë, Charlotte"; "Pius XI, Pope," not "Ratti, Achille"; "Pennsylvania State University," not "Pennsylvania State College."

Second, we may be more relaxed.

We then choose the author's name as it generally appears in the author's books. This means "Twain, Mark" and "Brontë, Charlotte"; "Unesco," not "United Nations Educational, Scientific, and Cultural Organization." For a great many books this demands less research; indeed, it requires only cataloging from the book in hand until one comes across another book by the same author but using a different form of the name. This is generally the approach of Lubetzky 1960, Paris 1961, and ALA 1967.

If the author changes his preferred form of name, we simply go along with him for the books published under the new name, and only for those books. This means we have some books entered under "Ratti, Achille," others by the same person under "Pius XI, Pope"; some under "Pennsylvania State College," others under "Pennsylvania State University." If a man writes under ten pseudonyms, we list under each heading the books he wrote under that name.

Thus, the disciple of the relaxed approach suggests that a uniform heading is not a uniform heading for an individual person, private or corporate. Instead, it is the uniform heading for an author. But a person may be as many authors as he (or she or it) wishes. If the noted physicist John Doe writes science fiction as Jeremiah Hoskins, he becomes two authors. This fact may be of interest in the biography of John Doe, but it need not affect the uniform headings for his works. In fact, the cataloger may actually hinder the finding of Jeremiah Hoskins' tales if he insists on entering them with heading "Doe, John," interfiled with treatises on theoretical physics. Catalogs are book-finding devices; they are not encyclopedias.

Brevity, we said, is useful in cataloging as, indeed, it is in all communication. Brevity applies to both the rigid approach and the relaxed approach. Dates of birth and death, occupation, place, title (excepting, of course, the nobleman whose title *is* his name)—generally all such things need to be added only if they serve to set off the heading from an otherwise identical heading for some other author listed in the catalog.

For corporate authors, brevity affects most of all our treatment of the parts of a corporate body. If the name of a part is so distinctive that it could pass as the name of an independent body—e.g., Association of College and Research Libraries—we may enter it directly under its own name. ALA 1949 (e.g., 99–102) allows this in certain exceptional cases; Lubetzky 1960 (33a and 47a), Paris 1961 (9.6–9.62), and ALA 1967 (70 and 78) make it a principle applicable to all subordinate bodies except those which are administrative, judicial, or legislative organs of government. In the same way, the subdivision of a part of a corporate body without an *individually* distinctive name might be entered directly under the name of the corporate body if *within the corporate body* this subdivision bears a distinctive name—e.g., "U.S. Bureau of Insular Affairs," not "U.S. War Dept. Bureau of Insular Affairs." ALA 1949 (75a) allows this for "bureaus and offices subordinate to an executive department of a government"; Lubetzky 1960 (33b and 47b) and ALA 1967 (69a and 79) allow it for all subdivisions of a corporate body (government or nongovernment).

Interlude on Evidence

Thus far we have talked of the relaxed approach and the rigid approach only in terms of what seems to be logic. Is there any concrete evidence? Two research projects appear to give some sort of answer; one relates to "No Conflict," the other, to Lubetzky 1960.

"No Conflict" was an administrative policy announced by LC, May 1, 1951. New personal name headings after that date were to be "established in the form given in the work being cataloged without further search, provided that . . . the name conforms to the A.L.A. rules for entry, and is not so similar to another name previously established as to give a good basis for the suspicion that both names refer to the same person."

After this policy had been in effect for ten years, Olivia Faulkner made a thorough and scholarly attempt to evaluate its success (published in LC's *Cataloging Service Bulletin,* 54 [Jan. 1960]). Almost conclusively the study shows that "No Conflict" produced great savings in cataloging cost with no reduction in usefulness of the catalog. Those few "No Conflict" headings which later had to be changed were generally changed because of information which became available *after* they had been put in use, i.e., even with an attempt to get the full and latest names of authors at time of cataloging, the changes would have had to be made later.

In an article in *Library Quarterly* (33:172–91 [1963]), Elizabeth Tate examined the relation of catalog entries prepared according to Lubetzky 1960 to the way in which books are cited in bibliographies and elsewhere. Broadly speaking, the study shows that a user equipped with such a bibliographical citation would have a better chance of finding his book under Lubetzky 1960 entry than under ALA 1949 entry. This, of course, would be expected to apply also to Paris 1961 which, on the whole, closely reflects Lubetzky 1960.

Now "No Conflict" and Lubetzky 1960 were both in large part products of the relaxed approach. It seems probable that they are practical as well as logical.

Rigid and Relaxed: Conclusion

So much for the rigid approach and the relaxed approach. The cataloger may choose one or the other, or he may choose a hybrid. The hybrid is what ALA 1967 and, indeed, most codes (and most catalogers as they apply the codes) do choose. But here lies danger. For each approach is an extreme. Like any extreme, either approach can be sharply defined, easily explained, easily understood. A compromise cannot be sharply defined. Look at the tangled web ALA 1949 (30) weaves when it chooses the "real" name and then excepts pseudonyms "fixed in literary history" but excepts "Twain, Mark" from this exception. Perhaps it is safer to choose one extreme or the other and then stick to the decision. Probably the relaxed approach is the easier to apply. If you choose the rigid approach, you will be tempted now and again to make an exception for the "convenience of the public."

Broadly speaking, the second objective and the rigid approach are more useful in the large research library, which often will have a great many books and many editions of those books by the same author and will want to list them all together in the catalog. On the other hand, the first objective and the relaxed approach may well be more useful in the public library and the school library. "A large library and a library used mainly by scholars," wrote Cutter (p.29), "may very properly show a preference for the real name; a town library will do well to freely choose the names by which authors are popularly known." Indeed, some small libraries reject the second objective.

It is true that the relaxed approach to changed names violates the second objective. But is the second objective always a useful objective even in the large research library? The second objective may be something on which the corporate author differs radically from the personal author, particularly the personal author of important literary works. Is it as likely that someone will want to see together entries for all that the library has by Pennsylvania State University (under whatever name) as that someone will want to see together entries for all the library has by Lord Byron?

Even if we limit the second objective to personal authors, it is hopelessly broad. The catalog does not list editions of "Hamlet" found in copies of Shakespeare's collected works or in unanalyzed sets of plays by various authors. Nor does it list material in the vertical files, pamphlets, and unanalyzed serials. More analytics might help; they would also cost money.

So the second objective raises a number of questions. To each the answer is arbitrary, depending largely on what we think is the "convenience of the public." For the two objectives are not themselves basic rules, nor are they absolute. Certainly they do not grant a logical escape from arbitrary decision. Indeed, the second objective is itself an arbitrary addition to the first, and its demand for a uniform heading leads to further arbitrary decisions.

Headings for Anonymous Works

We have been thinking of the conventional book with a single responsible author. What if the cataloger does not know who wrote the book? All that is left is to enter the book under title. But under what title? The title of an anonymous work may change as it goes through various editions. "The book of nature laid open" or "Popular philosophy"? "The Anglo-Saxon poem of Beowulf" or "The song of Beowulf"?

Just as with the various editions of the work of a single author (regardless of what different forms of the author's name each may bear), so with the various editions of an anonymous work (regardless of what different titles each may bear), the second objective demands a uniform heading. Otherwise, the catalog will not "relate and display together the editions which a library has of a given work," as Lubetzky 1960 phrases it (see p.28 above).

The application of the uniform-heading principle to entry for anonymous works has not been consistent. In Cutter and the ALA codes until 1967 there was a tendency to enter editions of modern anonymous works under their individual titles and to reserve the uniform heading for older anonymous works. Indeed, only the British in ALA 1908, when they differed from the Americans in their treatment of anonymous works with different spellings of the first word of the title in different editions (116) and in their treatment of the translations of anonymous works (118), and Lubetzky 1960 (62) applied the uniform heading to all anonymous works. Even Paris 1961 (6.1) allowed choice of the title "as printed in the book" or uniform heading, although it recommended uniform heading for "well known works, especially those known by conventional titles." ALA 1967 (Chapter 4) requires uniform heading for every anonymous work.

If a uniform heading is applied to a modern anonymous work, it is usually the title of the first edition, e.g., "The book of nature laid open," not "Popular philosophy." The uniform heading for an older anonymous work tends to be traditional or conventional and in the language of the original version when known, e.g., "Beowulf," not "The Anglo-Saxon poem of Beowulf" or "The song of Beowulf." In ALA 1949 the older anonymous works are generally considered as belonging to one of two classes: "Anonymous Classics" and anonymous religious literature. Parts of the Bible and most parts of other older anonymous works tend to be entered as subdivisions of the name of the whole work, e.g., "Bible. O.T. Job." Language, date of publication, and name of the version may be added as further subdivisions.

Of course, ALA 1949 division between older anonymous works and modern, and between classes of older anonymous works is unrealistic. The problem is not whether a work is old or modern or sacred or "classic"; rather it is simply a matter of dealing with all books whose authors are unknown. The answer is surely that of ALA 1967, uniform heading regardless of the age or status of the work.

How can the cataloger get the uniform heading? There is no choice of rigid approach or relaxed approach here. There is nothing to work from. If the cataloger has a modern anonymous work, how does he know it will go into another edition with a change of title? How does he know it is not another edition of something he has already cataloged under another title? Whether the work is modern or old, there is seldom, if ever, any such thing as the "real" title in the sense that there is a "real" name for an author. Almost always it is a matter of convention or of arbitrary choice between conventions. Perhaps the only thing to hope for is consistency. That, at least, he can have if he begins with a rather thorough statement of basic problems such as is found in ALA 1949, Lubetzky 1960, or ALA 1967 and then keeps a record of headings as he applies them.

So, as with books by single authors, the second objective demands a uniform heading for anonymous books. Yet, again, it does not show how to get that heading.

Arbitrary Entry

We began with the convention of author entry. We found that by the device of defining an "author" as "responsible for intellectual content," we could extend author entry beyond straight personal authors to corporate bodies and to compilers. We found, however, that it would stretch no further; indeed, we found that the concept of author entry would apply easily only to conventional books written by single authors, personal or corporate.

Then we examined the heading, the form the name of the author would take at the head of the author entry. We found that this heading must be a uniform heading for each author if entries for all the works of that author and all the editions of that author's works were to be kept together; this is the second objective. We found further that the second objective and the uniform heading are useful also with anonymous works. Finally, we found that choice of a particular form of an author's name for uniform heading or a particular form of the title of an anonymous work for uniform heading is generally arbitrary.

There remain several kinds of books for which no one author takes responsibility or for which catalogers do not use author entry even though there is an author. Yet these books must be listed under *something,* and if it seems good to keep together the entries for all editions of each book, that "something" must be a uniform heading.

Because the convention of author entry does not apply to such books, we must choose an arbitrary entry. There seem to be at least four broad classes of such works: (1) books with more than one author; (2) books whose authors change; (3) serials; and (4) books which have authors but for which catalogers' convention (to be distinguished from the popular convention recognized when we try to meet the "convenience of the public") settles on a non-author entry. We shall consider some of the problems involved in selecting an entry and a uniform heading for each.

Books with More than One Author

Ever since Cutter (218), codes—excepting ALA 1908—have preferred a heading naming only one author, probably for the reason offered by Cutter: "It leads to better arrangement." But which author if there are two or more?

Catalogers sometimes choose the entry by an extension of the idea of being "chiefly responsible for the intellectual content." Thus, Lubetzky 1960 (3), Paris 1961 (10), and ALA 1967 (3, 8, and 13)—and, under special conditions, ALA 1949 (4A)—generally call for entry under "principal author." Perhaps this is because he is considered "chiefly responsible." Otherwise, ALA 1949 (3A), Lubetzky 1960, Paris 1961, and ALA 1967 generally call for entry under the first named author; this, again, is a decision which, to some extent at least, may bring entry under the author "chiefly" responsible. But there is a taboo about the number three. If there are more than three authors, entry tends to be under title, unless, of course, the book's compiler seems to be "chiefly" responsible for intellectual content.

The principle of responsibility also applies to works prepared by one person for another. Entry is under the name of the person who assumes responsibility (Lubetzky 1960, 2a; ALA 1949, 3E; and ALA 1967, 16), even though he is, of course, not the "real" author.

The idea that a heading should name only one of several authors of a work is really unsatisfactory only in the case of famous teams such as Beaumont and Fletcher (in every play there were different shades of responsibility on which not even specialists are agreed) or Gilbert and Sullivan. (ALA 1949, 12A2, and ALA 1967, 19B Exception, call for entry under composer of the music.)

Books Whose Authors Change

We have been dealing with joint authorship planned by the authors. When the association was not planned, "responsibility" becomes more elusive. Often we are, indeed, dealing with change of author.

If, for instance, an anonymous work has come to be generally attributed to some author but the attribution never proved, ALA 1949 (31), Lubetzky 1960 (6), and ALA 1967 (2B) tend to make entry under the attributed author. For ancient and medieval books ALA 1949 does this even if the attribution is disproved or shaky.

Parodies, dramatizations, versifications, and the like are usually pretty clear cut; the "responsible" author is generally the later author. But with a translation, paraphrase, or adaptation the decision becomes subjective and arbitrary, much more so in ALA 1949 (20–22) than in Lubetzky 1960 (10) and ALA 1967 (7A) with the criterion that the new work must be rewritten in another literary style or in another literary form. Codes generally enter a translation under the original author, but Homer is not clearly "chiefly responsible" for a work such as Pope's Homer or Chapman's Homer.

With a reference work, on the other hand, the criterion of "responsibility" tends to vanish. Thus, ALA 1949 calls for entry of almanacs (5D) and directories published serially (5E) under title rather than compiler, and Lubetzky 1960 (5) would enter any work "issued in successive editions" with "different compilers or editors" under title rather than compiler, although he would, strangely enough, make an exception if the original compiler's name remains in the title. Thus Winchell's *Guide to Reference Books* is entered under neither "Mudge" nor "Winchell" but under title, while Blom's revision of Grove's *Dictionary of Music and Musicians* is entered under "Grove," not under title. This approach reappears in ALA 1967 (4A) where, among the examples, the *Directory of American Scholars* (1942) is entered under

"Cattell," but the 1963 edition is entered under title because Cattell's name appeared in the title in 1942 but not in 1963. ALA 1967 (6D1, note 11) specifically notes that "a person who is the author of a work issued periodically in revised editions is still considered to be the author even after his connection with the work ceases unless the new editions clearly indicate that the work is no longer his," with example *J. K. Lasser's Your Income Tax . . . revised by J. K. Lasser Institute* to be entered under Lasser. (It is a curious bit of pedantry that the Cattell *Directory* of 1963 had similarly been "edited by the Jacques Cattell Press," but the book is to be entered under title.) Finally, ALA 1967 (14B) requires that if the new edition of any work "clearly indicates that the work is no longer that of the original author," entry is to be under the new author, with example Winchell's *Guide to Reference Books* now entered under Winchell.

ALA 1967 (14B) with its consideration of the "original author" is clearly consistent with ALA 1967 (7A) which deals with rewritten literary works. Yet is this a practical approach to reference works? Is Grove or Cattell or Lasser truly the "responsible" author simply because his name appears on the title page? Does, indeed, the user think of a man or a title when he speaks of Grove's *Dictionary of Music and Musicians*?

There is another aspect: ALA 1949 was concerned about such works when "published serially"; Lubetzky 1960 introduced the criterion of "successive editions"; and ALA 1967 speaks of works "issued periodically in revised editions." Osborn called this sort of thing "pseudoserial" (p.18), and there is much to be said for his idea.

We move directly to the problems of serial entry.

Serials

What is a serial? Cutter (p.22): "A publication issued in successive parts, usually at regular intervals, and continued indefinitely." ALA 1967 (p.346) only adds detail: "A publication issued in successive parts bearing numerical or chronological designations and intended to be continued indefinitely. Serials include periodicals, newspapers, annuals (reports, yearbooks, etc.), the journals, memoirs, proceedings, transactions, etc., of societies, and numbered monographic series."

Perhaps the most striking thing about serials is their wide diversity; even the long catalog of varieties in ALA 1967 is not intended to be complete. ALA 1949 has individual rules for several forms of serial. Yet, for purposes of entry, the important consideration is something apart from form, as ALA 1967 (6) properly recognizes.

In all forms of the serial we are dealing with a publication (1) which appears in parts at intervals for an indefinite period of time and

(2) which may successively be prepared by different authors, compilers, or editors. We shall examine these two aspects.

First, publication in parts at intervals for an indefinite period of time at first seems completely to exempt serials from the two objectives, which we found satisfactory for the monographic works of personal authors. With serials we have a change in the meaning of terms. For instance, the various "editions" and "issues" of the monographic work of a personal author deal always with essentially the same text; only the type used to print that text has been changed in some way (see p.50 below). But when we speak of the "overseas edition" as contrasted with the "suburban edition" of a newspaper, or when we speak of the "June issue" and the "July issue" of a periodical, we are not dealing with the same text at all, and we may not even be dealing with the same title. The closest analogy might be the various chapters of a monographic work.

Yet the nature of serial publication seems to demand uniform heading. Only with this device can the librarian easily add to the library records each new issue as it appears. Only with uniform heading can the user easily find all that the library has of a serial.

Second, in the serial we are dealing with joint authorship or, more frequently, with works of composite authorship if we consider the individual issues or the bound volumes of these issues. We are also dealing with changing authorship if we consider the editor of each edition or issue as a compiler responsible for the intellectual content of the work. This would seem to indicate the title as the uniform heading for serials. Of course, if some person or corporate body assumes responsibility for the intellectual content of all editions and/or issues of the serial, the uniform heading could be the name of the person or corporate body.

There are still problems.

If the serial entered under title changes its title, which shall we use for heading, first title, successive titles, or latest title? ALA 1949 calls for latest title (5C); British practice calls for first title in ALA 1908 (121). Lubetzky 1960 fluctuated; first it adopted successive titles; then it allowed choice of any of the three; finally it again endorsed successive titles for "live" serials, latest title for "dead" serials. Paris 1961 calls for successive titles (11.5); ALA 1967 (6D1) also requires entry under successive titles.

There is, of course, something to be said for each choice. The first title or the latest title will be a uniform heading bringing together the record of all that the library has of the serial. On the other hand, entry under latest title demands frequent recataloging to keep the entry up to date; this will slow down serials cataloging and make it more expensive. Entry under first title might be cheaper and quicker;

Cutter called for it in all four editions of his *Rules*, although he did suggest the alternative of entry under successive titles. First title entry, however, might lead to entry under a title not actually held by the library, or to entry under some strange title, as for instance, "Daily Universal Register" for the London "Times."

What of "convenience of the public"? It seems probable that the user will come to the catalog with a reference to a particular article or passage using the title of the serial at the time when the reference was made. That is, entry under successive titles would best serve him. If the user wanted the bibliographical history of the serial, he would go to the appropriate bibliography—e.g., the *Union List of Serials*—because he would not expect the library to tell about issues of the serial it did not have any more than he would expect the catalog, instead of a bibliography, to tell him of books by Charles Dickens which the library did not have. It is true that the *Union List*, like any other bibliography, is not always completely accurate; but the cataloger does not check every printed bibliography for accuracy.

One user who may want in one place a complete list of the library's holdings of a particular serial is the order librarian. He may want to know if the library already has certain issues now offered for sale, or he may want to add new issues to the record. However, he would want this information only for *some* titles; the cataloger would have to provide the information for *all* titles in order to take care of his need. In any event, the order librarian has also available the order department's files, and he, like the "public" user, can always refer to a printed bibliography for help. So, for the serial entered under title, the successive titles would seem to provide the most useful uniform heading, even though it is not a uniform heading for the entire run of the serial.

For the serial with a corporate author, the heading presents its usual problems. Which name of the corporate body if it has changed names? We can only return to the relaxed approach vs. the rigid approach and to the suggestion that few of the users of the catalog may be as interested in finding all the works of a corporate author entered together as they would be in finding all the works of a personal author listed together.

But if we have adopted entry of a corporate body under its successive names, we have another problem. In effect, if not in fact, this solution results in a work with changing authorship, and for a work of changing authorship the current tendency seems to be toward entry under title (see p.35–36 above).

Corporate entry for serials raises the question of "convenience of the public." Whatever serials entry policy the cataloger adopts, the "public" probably will want consistency. The user may expect (if he has been around catalogs much) to find the formal reports of the business of a corporate body under the name of the corporate body, even though they may appear at intervals as regular as those of the *Atlantic Monthly*. But will he understand or be pleased to find that some of his scholarly serials are entered under title and some under corporate body? The *Papers* of the Bibliographical Society of America, for instance, he will find under "Bibliographical Society of America," while the *Library* of the Bibliographical Society (London) he will find under "Library." If he is a reasoning and a reasonable man, he may decide that this is because one serial has a distinctive title. Until 1967, however, his patience would have been further tried. He would have found *Studies in Bibliography* of the Bibliographical Society of the University of Virginia entered under "Virginia. University. Bibliographical Society." ALA 1967 (6) provides for entry of *Studies in Bibliography* under title.

The classic statement of the American position on corporate authorship is by Cutter (p.40): (1) "As a matter of fact, these bodies *are* the authors," and (2) "As a matter of convenience," both in the growing catalog and in "the service of the public," it is better to bring together in one place entries for "all the books connected with the name of a society or government." If all serials are listed under title, and you want to find "the publications of a German learned body you must look under Abhandlungen, Almanack . . . ," and Cutter then lists forty-one initial words possible in a German title. Many of these suggest serial publications. Cutter concludes his rather lengthy discussion: "Before the 'Rules for a dictionary catalog' were made catalogs seemed to me to be chaotic collections of empirical entries. I tried to find a few simple principles around which all desirable practices could be grouped. One of those principles is corporate authorship and *editorship* [italics mine]. I have as yet seen nothing to convince me that it is not a good one, since it corresponds to fact, inasmuch as societies are the authors of their proceedings and the collectors of their series . . ." (p.40).

"All the books connected with the name of a society or government" brought together under that name because of the "principles" of "corporate authorship and editorship." Have we here truly a logical decision, or is the "editorship" idea simply a rationalization of an arbitrary filing decision which solved the problem of many nondistinctive titles (in other languages no less than in German) interfiled with many other entries in a dictionary catalog?

Did, then, the serial tail wag the corporate dog?

In any event, since Cutter, corporate entry has flourished like the green bay tree and has brought under its shade all kinds of publications "issued" by corporate bodies. Yet in this very same period the definition of "author" has come more and more to rest on the idea that a book's author is responsible for its intellectual content. Many serial publications of corporate bodies even carry specific statements to the effect that these bodies do not assume responsibility for the content of the serials; the *ALA Bulletin* is one of these journals.

If we were to restrict corporate entry of serials to those serials for whose content the corporate body does assume responsibility, we should greatly increase the number of serial entries under title. Paris 1961 moved somewhat vaguely in this direction (9.11–9.12). ALA 1967 (6B1) calls for entry under title for a serial issued by a corporate body unless "the title (exclusive of the subtitle) includes the name or the abbreviation of the name of the corporate body, or consists solely of a generic term that requires the name of the body for adequate identification of the serial." The parenthetical subtitle exception to the exception allows entry under title for *Studies in Bibliography*; the "abbreviation" part of the rule brings the *ALA Bulletin* under the American Library Association; the "generic term" part is, of course, simply Cutter's dislike of *Abhandlungen*, etc. This is all very neat, but it is also a bit intricate. It is possible that the user of the catalog, and the public service librarian who tries to help him, will feel that there is more here about penguins than he really wants to know.

So much for serials. Rules and practices probably will continue to differ greatly from library to library regardless of what code a library professes to follow. In general, however, logic seems to suggest that ideally:

1. Serials entered under title should be entered under successive titles.
2. Corporate entry for serials should be restricted to those serials which report corporate business transacted or proposed by the corporate body, i.e., to serials for whose intellectual content the corporate body is responsible.
3. Personal entry for serials should be restricted to those serials for whose intellectual content a person is responsible.

In spite of logic and ideal solutions, it may well be that the solution most easily explained to users would be to enter *all* serials under successive titles. But Cutter's objections to this solution are still valid today.

Catalogers' Convention: The Non-Author Heading

Author entry, we found, rests on popular convention. People in the Western world have come to think of a book in terms of its author;

therefore, a heading consisting of the author's name will most easily locate the entry for the user. With some books, however, catalogers' convention ignores the author and chooses instead some sort of non-author heading. Such headings tend to bring out subject or form. There are at least four general groups: (1) Pseudo-Author Headings; (2) "Institution" Headings; (3) Form Headings; and (4) Certain Religious Works. Each will be considered briefly.

Pseudo-Author Headings

These generally have a subject approach. Some person or body other than the author is assumed to be more important than the author in the public's mind, and consequently this pseudo-author's name is used as heading. Thus, the catalog of a private collection (books, art, stamps, etc.) is entered under the name of the owner of the collection rather than the name of the cataloger (ALA 1949, 13). Reports of civil actions are entered under the party to the suit first named on the title page, in ALA 1949 (90B); under the party bringing the action in ALA 1967 (26C). Criminal trials are under the defendant, and admiralty proceedings relating to a vessel under the name of the vessel (ALA 1949, 90D–90G, and ALA 1967, 26C 1b).

"Institution" Headings

If we accept the principle of corporate entry and build the heading for a corporate author in the same way that we build the heading for a personal author, we have the name of the author followed by such additional qualifications (place, etc., just as dates, etc., for the personal author) as are needed to set off the heading from otherwise identical headings for other authors. This was precisely what Lubetzky 1960 (21 ff.) and Paris 1961 (9.4) sought to do, and there is logic and probably great usefulness in such a heading.

Cutter, however, had rejected headings directly under name for corporate bodies which lacked distinctive names: "a distinctive name is usually one beginning with a proper noun or adjective" (p.47). Instead, he entered such corporate bodies under place: "the place is not the author but is taken for heading that the entry may be more easily found" (p. 46). ALA 1908 and ALA 1949 kept Cutter's practice but abandoned Cutter's reason. Instead they tried to create distinctions between corporate bodies: "societies" as opposed to "institutions (establishments)" (ALA 1949, 91–92). Thus they moved away from the idea of heading determined by author's name to the idea of heading determined by organization of the corporate body and its physical equipment.

This has some curious results. It seems, for instance, logical and easy to accept "Boston. Public Library" (the ALA 1949 first illustration of an institutional heading); after all, there are many libraries which call themselves simply "Public Library," and the place will set them apart. Moreover, it is only a sort of conventional extension of the name, and in most places the Public Library is a subdivision of the local government anyway. But the same rule calls for "Pennsylvania. University," although the University is not a state university, and "Indiana. University," although the name is, of course, Indiana University. Finally, the distinction between "institutions" and "associations" does not always lead to Cutter's object of making an undistinctive name distinctive. We have, for instance, "Boston. Children's Hospital" but "Children's Aid Society, New York," although the institution and the association each has a nondistinctive name (Lubetzky Report, p.27). Also there is overly elaborate development of the rules. We make exception to the rule of entry under name to provide for entry under place and at once make exception to this exception to provide for entry under name if the institution has a distinctive name (ALA 1949, 91, 92).

"Institution" entry, as Lubetzky noted in his chapter on "the corporate complex" in the Lubetzky Report, is a splendid illustration of Osborn's statement ("Crisis in Cataloging"), "Elements of cataloging practice that were introduced for historical reasons come to be perpetuated without any understanding of why the rule was made." Lubetzky 1960 and Paris 1961 went back to the reason for the rule— simply to set apart like headings—and proposed that this purpose be accomplished in the same way it was accomplished for personal authors. Just as full forenames, dates, and titles are added (when needed) at the end of the heading for a personal author, so qualifications needed for differentiation (such as place) could be added at the end of the heading for a corporate author. This practice was logical and easy to explain.

But LC and the large research libraries using LC cards had built up long files of "institution" headings. They said they could not afford to pay for the cost of change. In the end, the ALA Cataloging and Classification Section yielded to this pressure because there is no point in writing a code which LC will not follow. "Institutions" remain in American cataloging practice, although we no longer call them such.

In ALA 1967 there is no artificial talk of "societies" and "institutions (establishments)." Instead, the introductory note to Special Rules on Geographic Names specifically states that in some cases geographic names are "used arbitrarily as the entry element of headings." The pertinent rules are ALA 1967, 98 and 99. Rule 98 deals with "Local churches etc."; examples: Baltimore. Third English Lutheran Church or Chicago. Hyde Park Union Church. Rule 99 deals with "Certain other corporate bodies": (1) educational institutions, (2) libraries, (3) galleries, (4) museums, (5) agricultural experiment stations, (6) airports, (7) botanical and zoological gardens, and (8) hospitals. Arbitrary place entry applies to such a corporate body if its name consists of "a common word or phrase" which may or may not be followed by the name of the jurisdiction "below the national level" in which it is located; examples: London. University *or* Pittsburgh. Carnegie Library.

Form Headings

Form headings have a long and interesting history. Early catalogs used them for anonymous books, catalogs, laws, dictionaries, pharmacopoeia, and the like. Panizzi's rules 80–90 allowed "Acadaemies," "Periodical Publications," "Ephemerides," "Catalogues," "Dictionaries," "Encyclopaedias," and "Liturgies." In this Panizzi was only giving sanction to long-established practice, although he and many of the catalog users questioned during the inquiry did not favor such form headings and urged instead that as far as possible each book should have its individual heading.

Since Panizzi, there has been a decline in the use of form headings. Paris 1961, however, may have a vague endorsement of them in its provision for a "suitable substitute for the title" if "author and title are inappropriate or insufficient for identification" (2.1c) and in its suggestion that "a uniform conventional heading chosen to reflect the form of the work" may be used for multilateral international treaties and similar works with "non-distinctive titles" (11.6).

In American cataloging the form heading hangs on as a subdivision of some corporate headings. Cutter (47) had suggested that laws be entered under the name of the country or state alone or with the name of the legislative body added as a subdivision, e.g., U.S. Congress. ALA 1908 (62) endorsed "U.S. Statutes." and, in one of its rare notes, defended the practice against the objection that it introduced "form or subject entries into the author catalog" on two grounds: (1) It would be "simpler" for libraries which have "extensive collections of laws," and (2) the names of legislative bodies change. A footnote gave LC practice, "U.S. Laws, statutes, etc.," and this expanded form was endorsed in ALA 1949 (84) and in ALA 1967 (20A). Similar form divisions allowed in American practice give such headings as "Catholic Church. Liturgy and ritual." ALA 1949 (116F) and ALA 1967 (29A1); "U.S. Treaties, etc." ALA 1949 (88A) and ALA 1967 (25); "South Africa. Constitution." ALA 1949 (85) and "Australia. Constitution." ALA 1967 (22A1) and so on.

Lubetzky 1960 had returned in large measure to the idea of author and title headings only, and he had provided entry under the simple name of the corporate body with (when necessary) the title of the book preceded by some kind of uniform title which would bring together all editions of the work. This, like entry of an "institution" directly under its name, LC and other research libraries rejected, and consequently the Catalog Code Revision Committee abandoned the idea. Alongside the old the new remained; ALA 1967 retained Lubetzky's idea of the uniform title. Thus we have such examples as ALA 1967 (101D):

> U. S. *Laws, statutes, etc.*
> [Shipping act (1961)]

or ALA 1967 (119A):

> Catholic Church. *Liturgy and ritual.*
> [Missal]

Finally, it may be worth noting that "South Africa. Constitution." and "Australia. Constitution." are completely form headings; neither element of either heading represents the author responsible for the document in question.

Certain Religious Works

We have seen (p.33 above) that the scriptures of most religions are anonymous and, therefore, are entered under uniform headings based on their titles. Such heading is applied also to certain religious works whose author is known, e.g., "Koran" and "Book of Mormon" (ALA 1949, 35D, and ALA 1967, 27A and 118).

Main Entry and Added Entry

Thus far we have been talking as though the catalog contained only one card for each book. This, of course, is what does happen in a union catalog. But in most catalogs there are several cards for almost every book.

Catalogers distinguish between what they call the "main entry," the "added entry," and the "subject entry." Broadly speaking, the main entry for a book is chosen according to the cataloger's rules of entry; the added entry takes care of another entry under which a noncataloger might look first, e.g., an entry for the editor of a book which the cataloger enters under title. We shall take up the subject entry in a later chapter; for the present we shall look rather closely at the main entry and added entry.

We begin with Cutter's definition of main entry (p.21): "The full or principal entry; usually the author entry . . . In a printed catalog it is distinguished from the added entries by having the *full* contents, which may be abridged or omitted in the subject entry, and all the bibliographical notes, most of which are left out in the added entry.

In a printed-card catalog the entries are of course all alike. Main entry in that case means the one on which is given, often on the back of the card, but sometimes by checks on the face, a list of all the other entries of the book (author, title, subject, reference, and analytical)."

Definitions in the ALA codes all omit the reference to the printed catalog, but otherwise they do not differ greatly from Cutter, although the 1941, 1949, and 1967 definitions are somewhat more expansive.

Main entry, then, meant something to the user in the beginning when printed catalogs were in style; now it means something to the user only in those catalogs where cards are typed and the catalogers choose (as with the printed catalog) to save money by making it fuller than other entries. In most catalogs, however, cards are printed or otherwise mechanically reproduced and, as Cutter said, every such card for a book is identical. Today we call this a "unit card." We add headings for added entries and subject entries to the top margins of unit cards for these entries; and we add a record of these headings (we call this record "tracing") to the lower margin or the back of the unit card which we use for main entry. Thus the main entry is important chiefly for its record of what the cataloger has done. Today main entry means something to the user only if (out of all the entries the cataloger has made for the book he wants) this entry happens to be the first he consults. But to the cataloger the main entry means almost everything. (Some libraries, of course, keep a record of tracings in some file other than the public catalog, e.g., in an official catalog or in the shelf list.)

To return to Cutter's definition: "usually the author entry." It is, indeed, conventional in our civilization to think of books in terms of their authors. But we found that this convention worked surely and smoothly only for a book with a single responsible author. For most other books we found that the entry is often arbitrary entry. For many books main entry is not "usually the author entry." This means that for these books the user may be most apt to find what he wants by means of an added entry under something conventional, such as an editor or a title, rather than by means of the main entry. Even for the book with a single responsible author, the user may remember only the title. It is not impossible that to the user main entry means nothing so long as there is *some* entry under which he finds the book he wants. This is an age of increasing multiple authorship and corporate sponsorship. Citation by author begins to lose favor in some areas. Finally, if we are to assume that the two objectives are simply a statement of the "convenience of the public," the two objectives are served just as well by added entry as by main entry.

Then why all the to-do about the choice of entry? Why not simply make main entry always under the one thing practically every book has: title? This would be the unit card. We could then make added entry for every other aspect of the book (author, editor, translator, joint author—what not?) that seemed worth bringing out. We could forget about arbitrary entry. Do we really need a code?

Main entry always under title would have its problems:

1. What form of the title? In the discussion of entry of anonymous works under title, we found that, at least for older anonymous works in several editions, a uniform heading was conventional. It seems, for instance, rather unlikely that anyone who wanted the King James Version of the Bible would find an entry beginning "The Holy Bible" or "The Sacred Scripture" as useful as the uniform heading "Bible. English. Authorized. 1611." The same thing may be true for books which are not anonymous. "The History of the Adventures of Joseph Andrews" or "Joseph Andrews," which would the user find more useful? We could, of course, simply copy each title exactly as it reads and then make added entry for the uniform heading. For many books this would result in a main entry really useful neither to cataloger (because he could find it only by consulting the added entry under the uniform heading) nor to user (because he would think of it only in terms of the author uniform heading). That is, the main entry under title might prove in some cases as useless and provoking as the main entry which is an arbitrary entry.

2. What form of author heading for the added entry? If we are to serve the two objectives, the matter of heading is still important. The answers are as they were before: If we want only the first objective, we may use the author's name as it appears in the book in hand. If we want also the second objective, we again need a uniform heading. There is here a problem with subject entry as well as added entry: If we have a book about "Huckleberry Finn," is the subject heading to be "Twain, Mark. Huckleberry Finn." or "Clemens, Samuel. Huckleberry Finn."—or, regardless of what we do with the author, do we call it plain "Huckleberry Finn" or "Adventures of Huckleberry Finn"? As long as we continue to think about books in terms of their authors, we shall have to pay attention to author heading.

3. For what shall we make added entry? What kind of authors? What kind of editors? What kind of titles? We can answer such questions readily only if we have a basic approach to choice of entry in general. Main entry always under title would, indeed, free us from debate about choice of main entry. Certainly it would free us from arbitrary entry, but it would not free us from choice of entry.

Who Did It? Short End to a Long Chapter

So much for author entry, title entry, and arbitrary entry and the heading which introduces each. Broadly speaking, author entry and title entry grow naturally out of the conventional thinking of the public; arbitrary entry is necessary because there is no one obvious author or title. Frequently, arbitrary entry is necessary only because it has always been done that way, and people think it would cost too much to change.

Entry and heading are a complicated business. Even if we could reduce main entry to one simple rule, such as entry under title, we should still need a code for added entry and heading.

4

What Does It Look Like?
Descriptive Cataloging

The heading will lead the catalog user to an entry. What will he find there? He will find what the cataloger thinks he needs to know about the book to decide if he wants to see the book itself. At different times and in different kinds of libraries the user has found different things in the descriptive part of the entry.

Early catalogs, almost till the end of the nineteenth century, were often content with a line or (sometimes) two to describe each book. For an obvious reason—cost—this was particularly true of printed catalogs. There were also some card catalogs in which the cards were not as tall as the 3 inch x 5 inch cards found in most catalogs today; in these catalogs, also, description had to be brief.

During the first forty years of this century, description became even more detailed. At least three influences may have been at work.

For one thing, there was the sister art of rare-book descriptive bibliography. A book may exist in several variant forms distinguished from each other by minute differences (see p.50 below). In a rare book these differences may mean financial gain or loss to the owner and intellectual gain or loss to the scholar. Bibliographers tended to describe rare books in some detail. It is perhaps only human to want to be "scholarly" with all books and to equate scholarship with detail. Research-library catalog cards blossomed with details. After all, who can tell when someone might need this particular bit of seemingly insignificant information? Get it down now, and the job will never have to be done again.

Then there was the decision to use the 3 x 5 card. Even on a 3 x 5 an extremist will begin to have doubts if his heading runs into two or three lines. Once he has his heading out of the way, there is left for description all that vast white space below the heading. He can even carry it over to a second card, and a third card was not, alas, unknown. Perhaps there is a Parkinson's Law about white space. Why is it there if not to be filled?

Finally, there was the distribution of LC cards. These cards were growing even more elaborate. Probably research libraries felt that cards produced locally should match them; the catalog would then be a symmetrical whole.

It all came to full bloom in ALA 1941, where for the first time every rule for every detail was set forth in brave array. The bloom was not long for this world. Osborn's "Crisis in Cataloging" attacked elaborate description with vigor; e.g., his vivid story of the moment of truth in a cataloging department when someone must decide if an "illus." is a "port." or a "front." and someone else must decide if the decider has decided correctly. The attack continued in the LC *Studies of Descriptive Cataloging* (1946), and with the publication of LC 1949 a retreat began. LC 1949 did not go as far as the *Studies* had shown was possible. Later, LC Supplementary Rules, particularly the decision of April 1951 (revised April 1952) calling for "limited cataloging" for certain kinds of material, continued the retreat. ALA 1967 (like LC 1949 before it) did not go as far in reduction of detail as the LC *Studies* had shown was possible; indeed, in some few areas ALA 1967 called for more detail. Manuals for smaller libraries and, more recently, manuals for processing centers have paid less attention to descriptive detail. Also, in some of the recent printed catalogs there has been emphasis on brief description. Some have even returned to the title-a-line ideal.

The Two Objectives

What is really necessary in descriptive cataloging?

Cutter's "Objects" say only that the catalog is "to assist in the choice of a book as to its edition (bibliographically)" and "as to its character (literary or topical)"; his "Means" note that this is to be done by "giving edition and imprint, with notes when necessary."

The LC "objectives of descriptive cataloging" (LC *Studies,* p.25, rephrased in LC 1949, p.7 and in ALA 1967, p.189) restate and develop Cutter's idea. The objectives are:

1. To state the significant features of an item with the purpose of distinguishing it from other items and describing its scope, contents, and bibliographic relation to other items.
2. To present these data in an entry which can be integrated with the entries for other items in the catalog and which will respond best to the interests of most users of the catalog.

With these two objectives, as with the two objectives for entry, we need to remember at least three things apart from their content:

1. They are not new; they are implied in Cutter's first edition (1876) and they have remained in American codes (implied or stated) ever since.

2. They are not in conflict with Cutter's concern about the "convenience of the public" (indeed the LC second objective mentions the user specifically). They merely state what catalogers feel best serves that convenience.

3. They will be most efficiently served by brief description. Each book need be described only as fully as is necessary to set it apart from other books, only as fully as will make it easy to find.

To be brief is obviously more necessary with the description than with the heading. That white space is tempting. Yet the cruel and stubborn fact remains that when a cataloger writes the description of a book, he is competing with all the other more fascinating things a reader can think of; and his plot is not quite breathtaking. Indeed, if he writes overmuch the reader may grow weary and fail to notice the one thing on the card he should see if he is to use this book wisely. So the card will be most useful if it is as brief as possible.

But How Brief?

We return to the question with which we began: What does the catalog user need to know about the book to decide if he wants to see it? Books may differ from each other in an infinite variety of ways. Even different copies of the same book may differ from each other. Yet in this infinite variety there is simplicity. Broadly speaking, books really differ in only two ways:

1. Books differ from one another if they contain different works.
2. Books containing the same work differ from one another if they are different editions, different printings, or different issues.

The first difference is generally obvious from the title of the book, although occasionally this is not the case. The second difference involves some definitions.

An edition consists of all the copies of a book printed from the same setting of type. A different edition may, or may not, involve revision of the text of the work.

A printing (sometimes called an "impression") consists of all copies of a book printed at the same time from the same setting of type. For most books printed before 1800, and for many printed since then, printing and edition are the same because the type was not left standing after it had been used. With the development of such devices as stereotype and electrotype plates and photographic printing, it became possible to have several or even many printings of an edition. A 1967 photographic reproduction of a 1601 book thus becomes a printing of the 1601 book although the original setting and even the type have long been destroyed.

An issue results when some important change is made in the book but the setting of type remains the same. For instance, a publisher may substitute a new title page with a different title and a more recent date for the older title page of a book which is not selling well.

An edition may consist of any number of printings, and each printing may consist of any number of issues.

How brief? It all depends. What differences between books are important to the catalog user? In a small public library, for instance, the edition of a book on physics may mean a great deal, but for a novel it may be enough to know that the library has five copies without bothering about the edition of each. In a large research library, however, the editions, printings, and issues of a great many books may be worth knowing.

The plain fact is that the user needs elaborate description of a book only if (1) he has seen (or intends to see) all copies of all editions, printings, and issues of that book, and (2) he cannot get at the book so elaborately described. Now the second condition should never be true. The first condition holds only if the user is making an intensive study of the history of the printing of the book, or if he is involved in critical analysis of the text, or if he is writing a detailed descriptive bibliography. For such a user it is enough that the author heading and brief description in the catalog call his attention to the book's existence in the library. He then asks for the book at the desk, and he can examine and describe it at his leisure.

Of course, now and then a person who is not a professional scholar wants to know something about the printing history of a book. He will be better served if the librarian sends him to a scholar's article, book, or bibliography—or even to the library's copy of the book itself —rather than if the cataloger has prepared an amateur's detailed description in the card catalog.

How brief? Whatever the answer, the cataloger shows it in the way he treats the title, the edition, the imprint, the collation, and the notes.

Title and Edition

On the catalog card the first paragraph beneath the heading begins with the title transcription (hereafter called simply the title). It generally follows the wording of the title on the main title page, and it has become conventional to begin it with an initial capital but to use capitals in the rest of the title only if they would be used in an English sentence. Like a sentence, the title closes with a period. The edition statement, if there is one, usually follows, and it is conventional to abbreviate it, e.g., 2d ed.

In a book printed today the title is apt to be short and crisp; in some books of today and in most books of earlier periods, the titles may be very long indeed. Cutter dealt vigorously with long titles (223):

> The more careful and student-like the probable use of the library the fuller the title should be—fuller, that is, of information, not of words. Many a title a yard long does not convey as much meaning as two well-chosen words . . . Other things being equal, that title is best which can be taken in at a glance. What has been said in defence of full titles may be true, that "it takes longer to abridge a title than to copy it in full," but it is also true that it takes longer for the printer to set the unabridged title, and longer for the reader to ascertain its meaning, and a long-title catalog, besides being more expensive, is more bulky and therefore less convenient.

Alongside his own rule, however, Cutter remarked that the ALA rule was "more rigorous" and that LC "usually gives the title in full, including the author's name." This ALA-LC approach, rather than that of Cutter, prevailed for over forty years; the reasons have been suggested above on pages 48–49. ALA 1908 (136) and ALA 1941 (225, etc.) developed in detail the idea of full and exact transcription of the book's title.

Only in 1946 with the LC *Studies of Descriptive Cataloging* was there a return to talk of transcription like that of Cutter: "fuller, that is, of information, not of words." The LC *Studies* attacked the logic of the full and elaborate title. The pamphlet also included (p.36–39) a report by Elizabeth Pierce of an experiment with 2504 main entries representing 198 titles: "No entry failed to be identified through the simplified cataloging when it would have been identified through full transcription." Full transcription of the book's title and imprint is, thus, not necessary to identify editions and issues. Indeed, "the element indicating reliably an edition or issue is not on the title-page but in the collation: the main paging." So even on the catalog card for a research library, the title may be abbreviated.

What is it safe to omit? Cutter properly warns that there is "no precise rule" (223). It seems logical to omit from the title anything which:

1. Repeats information elsewhere in the entry, e.g., the author statement. (We do tend to leave the author statement in the title if the author's name is given in a form different from that of the author heading or if there are two or three joint authors; cf. LC 1949, 3:6, and ALA 1967, 134.)

2. Is not needed to describe adequately the book's title or edition, e.g., what Cutter calls "puffs and many descriptive words which are implied either by the rest of the title or by custom of books of the class under treatment" (226). (ALA 1908, 136, however, called for a full title "usually"; LC 1949, 3:5, and ALA 1967, 133, moved back toward Cutter, allowing abridgment of "long titles" if this "can be done without loss of essential information." Speaking broadly, alternative titles and subtitles are often not as important for transcription as all ALA codes tend to make them.)

3. Is not necessary to prevent a false or inadequate understanding of the book's subject.

So it is safe to omit much. But precisely what? At this point, cataloging becomes an "art."

Thus far we have dealt only with the title on the main title page of the book. There may, of course, be other titles, e.g., a dust jacket title, a binder's title, a half title (also called fore title or bastard title), a series title, or a running title (sometimes called the headline). Finally, in early printed books, the title may appear (sometimes only) in the colophon. Generally these other titles have little significance for title transcription. If the title on the title page is scanty or inaccurate, the cataloger may wish to add something from these other titles. If there is no main title page, he will have to depend entirely on them for his title. (See ALA 1967, 132.)

Usually additions to the title are enclosed within brackets, but there is no general agreement about how to indicate omissions. The ALA codes require three dots for each omission, but there is much to be said for Cutter's contention (242, footnote) that the three dots are "suited only to bibliographies . . . The title in a catalog is not intended to be a substitute for the book itself and must leave some questions to be answered by the latter."

The Two Objectives Again

The two objectives are served by a brief title, but they require more than brevity. In the two objectives for description, as in the two objectives for entry, we have two concerns about the book:

1. The first objective looks at the book as an individual. Description applies to this book alone, noting "significant features . . . distinguishing it from other items."

2. The second objective looks at the book as one of a group of (perhaps similar) books; description must provide "an entry which can be integrated with the entries for other items in the catalog." That is, it keeps editions of a work together.

Just as with the two objectives for entry, here also there is conflict between objectives. The reason is the same: change. Two editions of the same work may have different titles. These different titles serve the first objective; they make the second impossible. The answer to the conflict of the two objectives for entry was uniform entry; the answer here is parallel: uniform title.

Cutter (222) and ALA 1941 (226) moved toward uniform title when they called for removal to the notes of title-page information which preceded the title of the book, e.g., the author's name or the series title. The LC *Studies* (p.30–31) proposed a conventional arrangement of parts of the title: title, subtitle (if present), author statement (where necessary), edition statement. This conventional sequence was to be secured by transposing the elements of the title-page title, if necessary. The same approach appeared in LC 1949 (3:2 and 3:4). ALA 1967, however, endorses a sequence of parts (130A) but allows transposition only for the subtitle (133H).

Editions or translations of the same work with different basic titles are another matter. American codes from Cutter to LC 1949 asked that the title follow only the title page of the book in hand and thrust down into a note the information that the work was once published under a different title. References would connect the different entries. Cutter (144) did suggest that works whose titles change in different editions "may be entered under the first"; although he concluded that "the most satisfactory method" was "to enter in full in both places."

ALA 1941 (p.371) had a footnote pointing out that in cataloging music "it is necessary to establish a conventional or standard title" which would occupy "the line between the author entry and the title . . . transcribed from the work in hand," although it had no examples with the rules for music. LC 1949 (9:2) required "conventional titles" for music "in order (a) to identify and bring together . . . all editions and arrangements of a composition and (b) to bring together in a systematic arrangement general and miscellaneous collections of a composer's works"; that is, in order to serve the second objective. LC 1949 cited as precedent "similar usages in the cataloging of . . . voluminous authors such as Goethe and Shakespeare and in the cataloging of editions of the Bible."

Libraries had, indeed, long been using the uniform title (generally within brackets in the upper right margin of the card), particularly for voluminous authors. Also, filing rules had been suggesting it, e.g., A.L.A. *Rules for Filing Catalog Cards* (1942), Rule 26.

Lubetzky 1960 proposed (strangely enough in a code for only author and title entry) that editions and translations with different titles be described under the original title, which thus became a uniform title. Similarly, he proposed to replace form subheadings, as "Constitution" and "Treaties," with uniform titles. In each case the uniform title would appear within brackets preceding the title-page title (7, 8, 42a, 42b).

The Catalog Code Revision Committee retained the form subheadings; but in ALA 1967 (100–102 and 119) the uniform title within brackets, preceding transcription of the title-page title, remains the rule for the various editions, translations, and the like of a work which appears under various titles. (Here, as in Lubetzky 1960, the rule appears as part of the section on rules for author and title entry.)

So much for the title and edition. A long and elaborate title is easiest for the cataloger; a short title constructed with care best serves the "convenience of the public." A uniform title would follow the logic of the two objectives, but we have never before 1967 required it in our rules, although we have often used it.

The Imprint

The title of the book, we said, is the name of the book. The title is thus, after the author's name, the first item in the identification of the book, just as the author's name is the first item in the identification of the author. Just as the author's name may require further detail—e.g., dates of birth and/or death—to set it apart from another author with the same name, so the title and edition statement (if there is one) may require further detail—e.g., imprint and collation—to set it apart from other editions or issues of the same work with the same title.

The imprint transcription (hereafter called simply the imprint) is an ironic contrast with the title in at least two respects:

1. Sequence is arbitrary and uniform: place, publisher, date.
2. Omission is not indicated by three dots; if there is more than one place or publisher the extras may be replaced by "etc."

In general, abbreviations are allowed somewhat more frequently in the imprint, but additions to the imprint, just as additions to the title and edition statement, have always been within brackets.

The imprint, like the title, has had its ups and downs. Cutter favored brief imprints, and ALA 1908 (150–57) did not insist on much more. The LC Supplementary Rule 12 (published alongside the 1908 rule) was quite detailed, and ALA 1941 (241–67) was elaborate indeed. The rules in LC 1949 (3:10–3:13) and ALA 1967 (138–41) were somewhat less elaborate.

What we prescribe for the imprint depends, of course, on what we think it can do. ALA 1941 suggested three functions: "1) to aid in the bibliographical identification of a book; 2) to indicate the source from which it may be procured; 3) to date the subject matter." LC

1949 (3:10) and ALA 1967 (138) added two more functions: The place "particularly if it is not a large publishing center" may suggest a "local viewpoint of the author"; and the publisher's name may "suggest a viewpoint or bias" or "the quality either of the subject matter or the physical make-up of the work."

If we accept these five functions as valid, we shall have fairly elaborate imprints. It seems probable that the buying-guide value of the imprint, even when it exists, is rather short-lived. Moreover, there is little evidence that many people do accept the imprint as a buying guide or as an indication of bias or quality in the book. Finally, if we take the two objectives seriously, only the first of these five functions (identification) and the third (date) are necessary to achieve the objectives.

Cutter's remarks (257) are still valid: "Imprints are indispensable in a catalog designed for scholars, that is, for college libraries, for historical or scientific libraries, and for large city libraries. They may not be of much use to nine persons in ten who use those libraries, but they should be inserted for the tenth person. But in the majority of popular city and town libraries neither the character of the readers nor of the books justifies their insertion . . . the year of publication is important under subject."

In the abbreviation of the imprint there are two major problems: (1) how many of several places and publishers to record, and (2) what dates to record.

With regard to places and publishers, there may be at least four variations: several places, one publisher; one place, several publishers; several places, several publishers; one place, one publisher. ALA 1941 has a rule for each. Yet if identification is all we want, it would seem logical to assume that in most cases the first place named and the corresponding publisher named were the most important to the people producing the book. So it would seem logical normally to record only these two, the procedures recommended in LC 1949 (3:10A) and ALA 1967 (138B1).

Likewise, there may be several dates. In addition to the title-page date, there may be on the verso of the title leaf the date of copyright and the dates of various later printings. Only two of these are important: (1) the date of copyright, because it tells the reader how long ago the work was actually written—a matter of critical importance with scientific or technical works but important also with some works of literary merit; (2) the date of the imprint or of the latest printing, because it is generally the date of printing the book at hand. Of these, the copyright date is, of course, the more important; but the other should perhaps also be recorded to avoid confusion. It is customary to record the copyright date in the imprint within brackets preceded by a "c" (surely a confusing thing for the reader unused to catalogers and their curious ways because "c" stands for so many words, among them "circa"). See ALA 1967 (141).

This discussion of several places, publishers, and dates has assumed that we need to record *some* place and *some* publisher. It may well be that neither is necessary, that only the date is helpful. Certainly, there are many bibliographies which record only the date of a book. Finally, as we noted under title, Elizabeth Pierce's report in the LC *Studies of Descriptive Cataloging* (p.36–39) showed that "the element indicating reliably an edition or issue is not on the title-page but in the collation: the main paging."

The Collation

For centuries a book as a physical object has been much the same. The basic unit of a book is a gathering of leaves produced by folding a part of a large sheet of paper, a whole sheet, or several sheets. The book may consist of one gathering, of several gatherings, or of many. If there is more than one gathering, they are arranged by signatures. The signature may be a letter of the alphabet in the lower margin of the top side of the first leaf of the gathering, and some, but not all, of the following leaves may also carry the signature accompanied by an arabic numeral to indicate the position of each leaf in the gathering. Or the signature may be itself an arabic number, or it may be an oblong black spot on the fold of the gathering. If the signatures are letters, successive gatherings are signed in the sequence of the alphabet; if the signatures are numerals, gatherings follow numerical sequence; if the signature is a mark on the fold of the gathering, the marks on the fold of successive gatherings will form a design on the spine of the unbound book. Each gathering is sewed at its middle fold to cords or tapes across the spine of the book, and these cords are attached to the covers. Or, if the book is thin enough, it may be stabbed (i.e., sewed through sideways) or stapled. In the paperback, and in other modern books, various adhesives sometimes replace this sewing process. There are, of course, other ways to bind a book.

The top side of a leaf is called the "recto"; the other side is the "verso." The recto of a leaf is a page, the verso is another page; each leaf, then, has two pages. In modern books, pages are generally rather carefully numbered, but numbering is sometimes in several series. For instance, the preface may be numbered in roman and the text in arabic.

The book may also contain one or more full pages of illustrative matter—or even folded sheets of illustrative matter. Sometimes these pages are included in the pagination of the book, sometimes they are separately numbered, sometimes they bear no numerical indication at all.

The cataloger tries to find out, usually by an examination of gatherings, signatures, leaves, pages, and illustrative matter, if the copy in hand is complete. In the collation he records the results of his examination. The collation is of considerable importance because in the LC *Studies* the Pierce essay showed that editions and issues are often and, perhaps, generally more reliably indicated in the collation than in the title or imprint. This is true of modern books; it is also true of older printed books. Title, edition statement, and imprint may often be the same for several books whose collation shows that they are differently made up and, therefore, are different editions or issues. On the other hand, title, edition statement, and imprint may be different—e.g., one may be called the "second edition" or have the name of a new publisher—for books whose collation shows they are otherwise identical or, at least, may be identical.

For older books and for rare books it is often customary to record the sequence of gatherings as well as (or instead of) the paging, and to describe the illustrative matter in some detail. In early printed books errors in pagination were frequent; indeed, printers seem often to have been almost deliberately careless about it. Thus the gatherings really had more significance, because as long as their signatures were correct, the book's leaves would come in correct sequence. Often, also, there was some variety in the illustrations in different copies of a book. In modern machine-made books there is, on the whole, greater uniformity.

The variety in early printed books and the tendency of descriptive bibliographers to describe this variety in detail may account, in some measure, for the elaborate collation prescribed in ALA 1941 (268–321), although these rules did not specify indication of gatherings. Cutter (276) had been perhaps too brief, but he had added the ALA practice (277–78). Broadly speaking, the ALA-LC rules have generally specified the last page number of each numbered sequence, often with some indication (within brackets) of unnumbered pages. Along with this tendency toward somewhat detailed statement of pagination, there has always been a strange inconsistency: All codes, even that of 1941, provide for a statement of pagination only with one-volume works. If the work is in more than one volume, only the number of volumes is recorded—unless pagination is continuous, in which case the one-volume attitude prevails. Also, if paging is complicated, there is a tendency simply to say "various pagings" (ALA 1967, 142A3) and, perhaps, to count and record within brackets the total number of pages. Apparently what is at issue is not some principle, but simply a feeling that even in elaborate cataloging sometimes too much work is too much.

Now collation, like everything else in cataloging, should be as brief as its purpose allows. What is the purpose of collation? There are at least two possible answers: (1) If the collation is, as often as possible, to identify editions, printings, and issues, then it must always account for every page of every gathering in the book. (2) If, on the other hand, the purpose of collation is simply to give the reader some general idea of how completely the subject of the book is treated, then it would generally be enough simply to tell the last page number of the major page sequence.

Perhaps the second statement of purpose is reasonably adequate for modern books in an ordinary library. In the Pierce study noted above, forty-nine groups of books each had two or more main entries of one title with "identical main paging." When these forty-nine groups were examined, forty groups "proved to consist of either issues, reprints, type-facsimiles or copies," although in each case "the title-page gave no hint of the fact that these groups were not of different editions." Indeed, the title pages often suggested, by changes in title or in imprint, that they were of different editions. Of the nine groups with identical paging which proved to be true editions, four groups were made up of books having varied editors, and two were published by corporate bodies. This kind of variation is generally noted on the title page of a book. So, of the forty-nine groups of books, the edition, printing, and issue of only two were not adequately identified by brief title and imprint and/or collation based on main paging.

This leaves for consideration the illustrative matter. ALA-LC rules (even LC 1949) have always made rather elaborate distinctions between types of illustrative matter and have even specified the order in which these various types are to be listed on the card. (See LC 1949, 3:14C, and ALA 1967, 142C.) But, if the book is generally adequately identified by title, edition statement, imprint, and collation, the only purpose which the statement of illustrative matter can serve is to tell of some kind of illustration which *would not be expected* in a book such as the title, edition statement, imprint, and pagination have described. For everything else the simple abbreviation "illus." would probably serve (cf. ALA 1967, C.1.a.).

After pagination and illustrations, Cutter, ALA, and LC asked for the height in centimeters. Various rationalizations have been offered in defense of this item, but the fact remains that Americans still think of measurements in inches (not centimeters) and that if height is to be of any help in locating the book, it should be part of the call number, where it will affect shelving and finding the book.

The final item of collation is the series statement. Its location seems a bit curious; one might logically have expected mention of the series in connection with the title or in the notes rather than as part of the collation paragraph, which is otherwise concerned only with the book as a physical object. LC 1949 (3:16) did indeed call it a "series note" but left this "note" in the collation paragraph. Only with ALA 1967 (143) do we call it "series statement," a term perhaps less misleading if it is to remain in the collation paragraph.

There are at least three kinds of series:

1. *Publisher's series.* The publisher may want to issue all his books in a particular subject area and/or in a uniform style with a general series name.

2. *Scholarly series.* Really this is only a special type of publisher's series in which some scholarly society or some university takes the place of the commercial publisher.

3. *Author's series.* An author may have all of his works in a particular subject area issued as a series.

Usually each book in a series is an individual work, i.e., a monograph independent of the other books in the series except that they all may deal with the same general subject. Sometimes, however, the work may occupy several volumes of the series. Sometimes the books in a series are numbered; sometimes they are not. Occasionally the numbering represents the sequence in which the books should be read; more often the numbering simply reflects the sequence of publication. (In such a case, the series-volume numbering may even be misleading: Volume 1 of a particular work may be the twentieth volume of the series and Volume 2 of the same work may be the fifty-first volume of the series.) Sometimes there is a general series editor who may or may not play a major role in developing and editing the series. Sometimes the same book may appear in two or more series, with a different volume number in each series.

Obviously the importance of different series varies greatly; it may be necessary to call attention to only some series. Probably there should be a statement for every scholarly series, every author's series, and every numbered series. Certainly there should be a statement for every series which is to have an added entry. With other series the need for a statement (and the need for an added entry) depends on two questions: Will the name of the series indicate to the reader the quality of the book and/or the book's general approach? Will this book be cited and called for by series rather than by author and/or title? If so, a series statement will be useful. But Eleanora Baer's *Titles in Series,* together with other lists, makes it unnecessary to have added entries for most series.

The form of the series statement has varied. Generally, if the series is described in the book itself, the statement is enclosed within parentheses; if series information is from another source, the statement is within brackets. In ALA 1908 (166) and in ALA 1941 (220a) the source of series information taken from the book but not from the title page was noted, but in LC 1949 (3:16) and ALA 1967 (143A) source need not be indicated. ALA 1941, 220 (1), requires that if the series statement "occurs in composition with the title," it is to be transcribed in the title instead of the series statement; LC 1949 and ALA 1967 would put most such statements in the series statement. Also included in the series statement are the author or editor if the series entry in the catalog is under his name and the number of the book within the series. Speaking broadly, the trend has been toward brevity and uniform sequence of elements in the series statement.

The Notes

In one or more paragraphs below the collation paragraph are the notes. Notes tidy up the entry. The heading, the title, the edition statement, the imprint, and the collation are each rather formal; tradition and need have set what may go into each and how it may be phrased. In the notes the cataloger tells anything more he thinks the reader should know about the book. Notes may thus deal with such things as the book's authorship, or the book as a physical object, or the book's relation to other books, e.g., editions and translations. In some instances, notes may even list the contents of the book or call attention to some special part of the contents, e.g., a good bibliography.

Perhaps most important, the notes may explain the subject of the book. The ALA and LC rules allow this only if the title is misleading or inadequate. Cutter asked for much more (284, paragraphs 3–4): "To direct the attention of persons not familiar with literature to the best books" and "to lay out courses of reading for that numerous class who are desirous of 'improving their minds.'" This meant "to characterize the best books only" while "dull books and morally bad books should be left in obscurity," although if "some of the poorer works" win "unmerited popularity a brief protest may be made."

The ALA-LC approach to subject matter is too restrictive; a book is read for its content, not for its appearance. Cutter's approach, however, could lead at its best to a subjective judgment of quality, at its worst to a form of censorship. Yet some sort of abstract is often more useful than many of the standard items in description. An impartial abstract like that found on a Wilson card or in *American Book Publishing Record* will best serve the user.

So much for what to write in the notes. How to write the notes?

It is a sad commentary on catalogers' originality and ability to use the English language that a list of notes used on LC cards has gone through two editions. Even ALA 1967 (144D) calls for "fixed forms for certain notes." Yet, common sense seems to require only that the cataloger write just what is needed, write it in his own words, and write it simply and directly. Above all, notes should be brief. Even ALA 1941 warned that "the ideal entry for the card catalog is the one in which everything . . . can go on a single printed card" (323, footnote).

The Tracing

The tracing is the final paragraph of the card, and it is customary to list subject headings first and then the added entries. LC 1949 (3:25) and ALA 1967 (151A) have an arbitrary sequence for all items in the tracing; possibly an alphabetical arrangement might be more useful if the tracing is, indeed, to be used for recovering from the catalog all cards with added headings for the book when they are needed.

On LC cards the tracing comes at the foot of the card; in some libraries with typed cards the tracing may even come on the reverse of the card. The information implied in the subject headings listed in the tracing could be quite useful to the reader, if it were specifically presented as information. Among the notes could be one beginning with some such phrase as "For other books on this subject in the library look under," and then would follow the subject headings listed in the tracing.

Serials

Thus far we have dealt with description based largely on a single main title page and a single collation. With a serial, however, we may have any number of main (and other) title pages each with its own information, and we have a collation which is (at least intended) to run on forever. Only after a serial has finally died can the cataloger describe it in peace. Meanwhile many serials flourish, and the cataloger must do something about them before they run him down. What?

Description of a serial can be elaborate indeed. The ALA-LC rules for serials (e.g., ALA 1967, 160–72) and the bubbling enthusiasm of Harriet Wheeler Pierson and Mary Wilson MacNair would send the cataloger on a long and intriguing search in all sorts of out-of-the-way places, and he would end up with a complete history of the serial from its birth. All this he would then record in detail, and he would leave a spot for the future, e.g., an incomplete imprint date such as "1964– " or a bleakly blank collation such as simply " v." Of course, he would need notes. LC 1949 and ALA 1967 list some sixteen different kinds of notes (there are, no doubt, others), such things as frequency of publication, report year (if it is an annual report), duration of publication, issuing bodies, various editors and their length of service.

But a serial is a living—therefore, a changing—creature. This means that anything the cataloger writes about it today may have to be changed with the next issue tomorrow. This eats time. In 1953 in LC only some 65 percent of serial descriptive cataloging went to original cataloging; about 35 percent went to recataloging (Osborn, *Serial Publication*, p.155). Moreover, much of the history of serials is often already recorded in printed bibliographies, such as the *Union List of Serials*, and elsewhere.

Finally, there is the user of the catalog. What will he want? Probably he will ask only one thing: Does the library have the March 1955 issue of *Suchandsuch*? He will not much care if for two months in 1934 this periodical was not issued, or called itself *Suchandso*, or was edited by John Joseph Biblos, or was issued by the American Society for the Preservation of Whatnots, or was published in Philadelphia instead of New York. And he will not be happy if the discovery of all these fascinating facts has held up the cataloging of *Suchandsuch* so long that the card is not even in the catalog.

Even to answer this one question about the March 1955 issue would mean constant change of the catalog cards for *Suchandsuch* if the addition of each issue was recorded. For this reason, catalogers may show what the library has with some phrase such as "June 1932–date" and/or "v.2, no.5–date." For clarity such a statement should perhaps be introduced by a phrase such as "Library has." Perhaps even better is to establish a central serial record; then the catalog will need only a card for each title of the serial with a reference to the central serial record for holdings.

So much for what in the serial would correspond to title and collation. Imprint is, of course, useful on a serial card if the title is the same as that of another serial already listed in the catalog. Probably notes are needed only (1) if the title fails to make clear what is the subject of the serial, or (2) if the serial succeeds, or is succeeded by, or has some other relationship to, another serial.

Effective descriptive cataloging of serials depends on at least two imperatives: (1) omit most details that can change—e.g., editors, publishers, frequency, and (2) catalog only what the library has—not what would make a "complete" set.

Brevity Is the Soul of Wit

For too long, description of books has meant worship of the main title page. Catalogers have copied out trivia in detail or replaced them with three dots per trivium. If they have found useful information elsewhere in the book, they have carefully tucked it within brackets, although that was also what they did with information from outside the book. They have preserved the order of items in the title-page title, although that order reflected only the printer's care for the appearance of the title page or the printer's whim; never did that order reflect concern about how the title would best be recorded and most efficiently used in the catalog. Only in copying the imprint has the cataloger imposed a uniform sequence of items. Yet, none of these things—three dots, brackets, title-page order of items—interests the catalog user. Two of them—the two meanings of brackets and the two kinds of order—he does not understand. Even if he did understand, how could he tell them apart? Possibly on occasion the title-page title even confuses his search.

Most of the books in a library are ordinary books, and most of the users of a library are ordinary people. They want books for information or for entertainment. All they really need to know about a book is: (1) What is its brief title? (2) What is it about, if the title does not tell? (3) How up to date is it? (4) How long is it?

They get all this if the cataloger describes the book briefly.

5

What Is It About?
Subject Entry

Main entry and added entries help the user find a book if he knows the name of some person or corporate body connected with the book or if he knows the title of the book. But what if he wants a book on frogs, and he does not know the name of anyone who has written such a book? In the dictionary catalog he will find the book entered under the subject heading *Frogs*. It has not always been this way.

Subject arrangement in early catalogs was common, but the subjects were often very broad, e.g., *Law* or *Theology*. Generally they seem merely to have reflected the arrangement of the books on the shelves. In such a catalog one might have found the book on frogs under something like *Natural History*. Later the genuine classed catalog with systematic subdivisions (see p.3 above) became popular. Here the user might find the book on frogs listed logically under one of the subdivisions of subdivisions of *Zoology*, but unless he was familiar with the classification scheme used, he would not even know where in the catalog to find *Zoology*, let alone such a minute part as *Frogs*. So classed arrangement generally requires some sort of index if it is to be used easily; perhaps the user would find *Frogs* in the index.

With the publication of Cutter's famous catalog of the Boston Athenaeum, beginning in 1874, and with the successive editions of his *Rules for a Dictionary Catalog* (first 1876, fourth 1904), what we call "specific entry" (see p.66 below) and the "dictionary catalog" (see p.3 above) gradually took over the libraries of America. When LC adopted Cutter's approach and made tracings for such subject headings on LC cards, the conquest was complete. Since Cutter there has been no major change in American library subject heading theory. Haykin's *Subject Headings* sought only to explain and bring some

65

system to what LC practice had done with Cutter's approach to the dictionary catalog. In such a catalog the user finds the book on frogs entered directly under *Frogs*.

Before Cutter there had been two hundred years or more of experimentation. The classed catalog, the alphabetico-classed catalog (see p.3 above), form headings (see p.43 above), catchword headings and subject-word headings derived from the titles of books (see p.67 below), the index as used both with the classed catalog and in published general indexes such as Poole's—each played its part, and fragments of each (sometimes well concealed) remain imbedded in our thinking about subject analysis today.

First we shall look at Cutter's contribution.

Cutter

Cutter's basic ideas appeared in the 1876 edition of his *Rules,* and they were repeated with relatively few changes in later editions. Among them are the following:

1. Specific Entry (No.66 in 1876 and No.161 in 1904): "Enter a work under its subject-heading, not under the heading of a class which includes that subject."

2. Cross References (No.71 in 1876 and No.168 in 1904): "Of two exactly synonymous names choose one and make a reference from the other."

3. Compound Headings (No.76 in 1876 and No. 175 in 1904): "Enter a compound subject-name by its first word, inverting the phrase only when some other word is decidedly more significant or is often used alone with the same meaning as the whole name."

4. Subdivision (No.199 in 1876 and No.340 in 1904): "Under subject-headings group titles topically when it can be done, otherwise arrange them by the authors' names."

5. Syndetic Aspect (No.85 and 86, further defined on p.15 in 1876; and No.187 and 188, further defined on p.23 in 1904): "Make references from general subjects to their various subordinate subjects and also to coordinate and illustrative subjects [and] make references occasionally from specific to general subjects."

6. The User (p.6, on cataloging in general, 1904): "The convenience of the public is always to be set before the ease of the cataloger . . . When [the public's] habits are . . . deeply rooted, it is unwise for the cataloger to ignore them even if they demand a sacrifice of system and simplicity."

The Two Objectives

Cutter's rules for subject entry rested on two of his "Objects":

1. To enable a person to find a book of which the subject is known, and
2. To show what the library has on a given subject and in a given kind of literature.

With these two objectives, as with the two objectives for author and title entry and with those for descriptive cataloging, we have again the dual approach to the book (1) as an individual and (2) as one of a group of books.

The first objective will be best served only if we have entry under the specific subject of the book, the one subject with which it truly tries to deal. With the second objective (as with the second objective in the other pairs) conflict comes. For one thing, the subject of a book may have different names in other books. For instance, one of the predecessors of "specific entry" was "subject-word-entry," an "entry made under a word of the title which indicates the subject of the book" (Cutter p.19 and No.151). William F. Poole's catalog of the Boston Mercantile Library (1854) was a dictionary catalog in that author, title, and subject entries were interfiled; but the subject entries were subject-word entries. This meant that the synonymous terms used in different titles scattered the entries for books on the same subject. Cutter felt it necessary to state (No.172): "Enter books under the word which best expresses their subject, whether it occurs in the title or not."

Even if the cataloger chooses the name which "best expresses" a subject and then always uses only that name for that subject, conflict is possible. The name of a subject, like the name of a person, may change, e.g., *Ague* and *Malaria*. The answer to this conflict of the two objectives is again the same: the uniform heading. This solution, of course, calls for cross references from rejected terms to the term chosen (Cutter's No.168, cited p.66 above). Finally, these two objectives, like the other sets of objectives, do not ignore the user; they simply state what is assumed to be the user's basic need.

Specific Entry

Precisely what do we mean by this term? We have noted above that the first objective calls for specific entry. Cutter felt that specific entry is "the main distinction between the dictionary catalog and the alphabetico-classed" (p.67). But is it? The alphabetico-classed catalog consists of alphabetically arranged broad subjects, each subdivided alphabetically into its parts and subparts (see p.3 above). In such a catalog a book on frogs would have the subject heading:

Zoology—Vertebrates—Amphibians—Frogs.

Zoology would come along with other headings beginning with "Z" rather than, as in the classed catalog, alongside, perhaps, *Botany*; *Vertebrates* would come alphabetically in the "V's" among the other subdivisions of *Zoology*; and *Frogs* would come in the "F's" among the various subdivisions under *Zoology–Vertebrates–Amphibians*, rather than where it might belong in a logical sequence of amphibians.

Consider again the alphabetico-classed subject entry:

Zoology–Vertebrates–Amphibians–Frogs.

Surely this is as specific as the simple subject entry:

Frogs.

The difference, then, between the dictionary catalog and the alphabetico-classed catalog lies not in the specific entry but in the way the user gets to that specific entry. That is, the difference is not in the entry but in the heading. One heading begins with a major class and leads the user through the subdivisions of that class down to the specific subject of the book; the other heading is only the name of the specific subject of the book. Wyllis Wright has suggested the phrase "direct and specific entry." This is, indeed, a more accurate description of what Cutter had in mind.

In the discussion of subject headings, "specific" is often used as if it meant "narrow" (in contrast with "broad" or "general") subjects; Cutter himself used the word in this sense in his Rule 188, cited above on page 66: "Make references occasionally from specific to general subjects." Yet elsewhere (p.19) Cutter remarks that "whenever a book treats of the whole subject as a class it is specifically entered under that class. A theological encyclopedia is specifically entered under *Theology*." If a book deals with the world, then *World* is the specific subject of that book. A specific entry is sometimes for a broad subject, sometimes for a narrow subject. It all depends on the subject of the book.

It may be that direct and specific entry does not always serve the user well. If, for instance, in a small library there are five French dictionaries, will it help the user to show in the subject entries that one is in French only, that the other four are French-English, that one of these four is intended only for the use of beginning students of French, and that another of the four contains also an English-French section? Will the user jump to the conclusion that the first entry he chances on is the only French dictionary the library has? Would it have been better in this library simply to have had an entry for the general subject of French dictionaries? (See also p.85).

Again, apart from literary works, the chief reason for writing a book—if it is a good book—is that the author thinks he has a brand-new subject or at least a brand-new way of looking at his subject. How can we give a useful direct and specific entry to this subject? Perhaps no one except the author knows the subject exists. The extent to which the direct and specific entry for such a subject is correct is precisely the extent to which the user will not think of looking for it. Cutter, of course, recognized this problem but felt that such subjects "must attain a certain individuality . . . and be given some sort of *name*, otherwise we must assign them class-entry" (p.67). This, of course, would mean to mix class entries which are direct and specific with class entries which are not. What becomes, in this case, of the second objective and uniform heading? Would the user think to look for this nameless subject under the entries for the class which contains it—particularly if he had been informed of the rule of direct and specific entry? Then, if this new subject does someday get "some sort of *name*," must the cataloger plow through all the class entries and pull out the cards which should bear direct and specific entry for the new name? For that matter, how do we know at what point the new subject has, in truth, received "some sort of *name*" which we can accept?

So much for direct and specific entry and a few (but not all) of its problems.

Direct and Specific Subject Headings

The idea of the dictionary catalog is pleasantly concrete: It is simply an alphabetical file of names—the names of authors, the names of books (i.e., their titles), and the names of subjects.

With the name of an author or the name of a book, there is a word or words—something in black and white—to begin with. All the cataloger has to do is to choose which names he will use and how he will arrange the words of each name to form a heading. This is sometimes difficult but it is seldom impossible. Indeed, the possible choices are so few that he can get (and later find when he needs them) most of them into a code for author and title entry and headings. Because the user often begins with the same word or words as the cataloger, he may often end up with the same answer.

With the name of a subject, the cataloger has an idea—not something in black and white—to begin with. As to a word or words for the idea, he must think them up himself. He deals, that is to say, not merely with the arrangement of words but with the choice of the words themselves. The user also begins with an idea, and he must turn it into a word or series of words and then arrange the words. The chance that his answer (i.e., his subject heading) will differ from the cataloger's answer is great.

There are at least two basic kinds of direct and specific subject headings: (1) Single-Noun Heading and (2) Compound Heading, consisting of one or more nouns and (sometimes) one or more adjectives. Each kind may sometimes have subdivisions.

We shall consider each kind of heading briefly, and then we shall look at subdivision.

SINGLE-NOUN HEADING

This is, of course, the simplest kind of subject heading, and it creates few if any problems: *Botany, Gallows, Ethics.*

COMPOUND HEADING

The variety of combinations is almost infinite. Cutter (p.71-72) listed five (the numbering is my own):

1. A noun preceded by an adjective, as *Ancient history, Capital punishment.*
2. A noun preceded by another noun used like an adjective, as *Death penalty, Flower fertilization.*
3. A noun connected with another by a preposition, as *Penalty of death, Fertilization of flowers.*
4. A noun connected with another by *and* as *Ancients and moderns.*
5. A phrase or sentence, as in the title "Sur la regle Paterna paternis materna maternis," where the whole phrase *Paterna paternis materna maternis* would be the subject.

Haykin's list (p.21-25) is somewhat more detailed (the numbering is my own):

1. Adjectival headings (equals Cutter 1 and 2 above), as *Agricultural credit* or *Electron microscope.*
2. Phrase headings (equals Cutter 3 and perhaps Cutter 5 above?) formed of two nouns with or without modifiers, connected by a preposition or conjunction, and used to express an other than additive relationship, as *Women as authors, Church work with youth, Divine right of kings.*
3. Compound headings (in general, equals Cutter 4 above) two or more coordinate elements joined by *and*, as *Literature and morals, Bolts and nuts, Weights and measures.*
4. Composite forms (actually only variations of the others, particularly Haykin 1), such as two adjectives used to define a noun—*Open and closed shop*—or one adjective used to modify two nouns—*Tobacco jars and boxes.*

Confronted with this bewildering array of combinations, we are compelled to accept every one of them if we accept the principle of direct and specific entry. How are we to express such a combination in a direct and specific heading? Exactly as it stands? Or with some sort of inversion?

With considerable misgiving Cutter wrote his Rule 175 (see p.66 above, No.3): "Enter a compound subject-name by its first word, inverting the phrase only when some other word is decidedly more significant or is often used alone with the same meaning as the whole name." As examples he listed *Special providences* and *Providence, Proper names* and *Names*. He added that "it must be confessed that this rule is somewhat vague and that it would be often of doubtful application . . ." It is indeed. How do we know if a word is "decidedly more significant"?

Haykin, like most other American catalogers, accepted the rule and added two types of heading to his list:

5. Inverted adjectival headings, to bring the noun "next to other headings beginning with that noun, or because the adjective is used simply to differentiate between several headings on the same subject."

(What adjective is not so used?) His examples are *Art, Medieval* and *Geography, Economic*.

6. Inverted phrase headings. Although "uninverted phrase headings are to be preferred" and "most readers would not look under the inverted form," inversion is used "when the first element in effect qualifies the second and the second is used in the catalog as an independent heading." This is "equivalent to subdivision," but it is used instead of subdivision "to preserve the integrity of the commonly used phrase."

(Does not inversion itself destroy the "integrity" of the phrase?) Examples are *Plants, Protection of* and *Debt, Imprisonment for*.

So we accept the compound heading if we accept direct and specific entry. We sometimes use an inverted form, although this is, indeed, as Haykin said "equivalent to subdivision." Suppose we look at subdivision.

Subdivision (Cutter)

Subdivision is the mark of the alphabetico-classed catalog. As such it is to be shunned; and yet we have Cutter's Rule 340: "Under subject-headings group titles topically when it can be done, otherwise arrange them by the author's names." True, this is one of a group of rules on arrangement rather than on theory of entry. It is less easy to plough through a long list of authors arranged alphabetically under a subject than, under that subject, "to run over five or six [sub]headings given by another man, and representing that man's idea of classification." For "the object aimed at—enabling the enquirer to find quickly the book that treats of the branch of the subject which *he* is interested in—is attained if the mass of titles is broken up into sections containing from half a dozen to a score" (Cutter, p.123).

That is to say, he is here most interested in "convenience of the public." As samples of appropriate subdivisions he offers *Bibliography, History, Dictionaries, Periodicals, Natural history, Description and travels,* and the like.

Yet the line between subdivision by topic to help the user find entries, and subdivision by topic to get to the specific subject (as in the alphabetico-classed catalog) is thin indeed. Cutter himself referred to these arrangement subheadings as representing the cataloger's "idea of *classification*" (see above; the italics are mine).

Further subdivision of these subdivisions, he suggested, should be chronological for "groups or subjects of a historical character" (Rule 341). Particularly intriguing is Rule 343: "When the titles are numerous under a subject heading divide them, but avoid [further] subdivision." The last clause ("avoid [further] subdivision") apparently again tries to draw the line more closely between what he has in mind (headings for direct and specific entry) and the headings in an alphabetico-classed catalog. In two parallel columns he then lists possible subdivisions under the name of a country: "The second is the dictionary plan pure and simple: the first is a bit of classification introduced for special reasons into a dictionary catalog" (his own catalog of the Boston Athenaeum). A few of the headings which might result from these two lists are below:

> *Boston Athenaeum:*
> > United States—Literature—Ballads and songs
> > United States—Language—Dialects
> *Dictionary Catalog:*
> > United States—Ballads and songs
> > United States—Dialects

In another way Cutter sacrifices direct and specific entry to arrangement: "Often it will be expedient to combine those [sub]divisions in which there are very few titles into one more general; thus *Botany, Herpetology, Ichthyology, Zoology,* would join to give *Natural history* a respectable size" (p.127). In both lists each of these five terms appears as a possible direct subdivision under a country's name.

So Cutter allowed subject heading subdivision; but he tried to allow it only to make the entries under a subject heading easier for the user to find.

One question remained: If the original subject heading could be subdivided in *any* way, was it *truly* the direct and specific subject heading for the books listed under it?

Subdivision (Haykin)

Haykin sought only to refine and expand Cutter's approach. Subdivision, he suggested, "is distinguished from qualification in that it is ordinarily used not to limit the scope of the subject matter as such but to provide for its arrangement in the catalog." Subdivision should thus "as far as possible be limited to the form in which the subject matter is presented and the time and place to which it is limited" (p.27).

Even thus closely hedged, subdivision has problems. Form subdivision, for instance, he says, is based on "form or arrangement" and "it represents what the book is, rather than what it is about" (p.27). As an illustration of what he has in mind, he then lists several "form subdivisions" under the heading *Agriculture*. A few of these, accompanied by Haykin's explanations, are below:

> Agriculture—Abstracts.
> —Periodicals.
> —Bibliography.
> —History.
>> For the history of the progress of the art and science of agriculture.
> —Study and teaching.
>> For works on schools of agriculture and methods of teaching the subject.
> —Terminology.
>> For discussions of the vocabulary of agriculture and lists of words not of the nature of dictionaries.

Of these subdivisions, *History, Study and teaching,* and *Terminology* seem hardly to "represent what the book is, rather than what it is about" if we accept Haykin's definitions of these three terms. The others are, perhaps, "form" by his definition. But form divisions are to be found in many classification schemes; if we keep them at all, do we retain an "alphabetico-classed" approach? At least some of these headings could be phrases, e.g., *Agricultural abstracts* might do as well as *Agriculture—Abstracts.*

Subdivision by place brings the problem of Direct Subdivision and Indirect Subdivision:

> *Direct Subdivision:*
> Art—Paris (*Not* Art—France—Paris)
> *Indirect Subdivision:*
> Reformation—Germany—Palatinate (*Not* Reformation—Palatinate)

Indirect subdivision "assumes that the interest and significance of certain subjects are inseparable from the larger area" (p.30), while direct subdivision "offers but one problem: how to bring to the reader the material on one state, province or country when it is scattered under names of cities, counties, lakes . . . within it" (p.31). That is, the advantage of indirect subdivision is that it is more thoroughly alphabetico-classed than is direct subdivision. The difficulty of defining precisely which kinds of subjects require indirect subdivision (not the fact that indirect is alphabetico-classed) has led to greater use of direct subdivision.

Subdivision by time Haykin illustrates with headings such as the following:

> U.S.—History—Queen Anne's War, 1702–1713.
> (with cross reference from *Queen Anne's War,* 1702–1713)
> U.S.—History—Revolution
> (with cross reference from *American Revolution*)
> Franco-German War, 1870–1871
> (with cross references from *France—History—Franco-German War,* 1870–1871
>
> and
>
> *Germany—History—Franco-German War,* 1870–1871)

Of these headings only one is truly direct and specific: *Franco-German War,* 1870–1871. This heading Haykin defends not for that reason but because it represents a war "in which two or more countries participated" (p.34)—that is, because it cannot properly be entered as a subdivision of any one main heading. American Revolution and Queen Anne's War, on the other hand, are subdivisions because "wars, other than those of world wide scope, in which the United States (or the American Colonies) took part are entered under United States" (p.35). We have then, in essence, the following rules for time subdivision as it relates to history:

History is a subdivision under a heading for the name of a country.

History is itself subdivided by periods of time, with a name given to the period if it has one.

Exception: Wars in which two or more countries participated are entered directly under their own names.

Exception to the exception: Such a war "other than those of world-wide scope" involving the United States is entered under *U.S.*

Further exception (no example above): "Battles are entered not under the war heading, but under their own names" (p.35).

"Subdivision by topic" is the title of the rather curious section with which Haykin closes his chapter on subdivision. He suggests the following examples of subdivision by topic:

Heart—Diseases.
Insurance, Social—Research.
Social Psychology—Research.

Such headings, he suggests, "resemble alphabetico-classed headings in their outward form only," because they are used when "a convenient phrase form sanctioned by usage is lacking" or when "it is desirable to conform to an existing pattern" (p.36). A heading such as *Heart diseases,* for instance, would separate in the catalog "entries for works on the heart in general, on abnormalities of the heart, and on the diseases of the heart." Yet surely this kind of defense of "subdivision by topic" is a defense of the alphabetico-classed approach.

So a direct and specific subject heading may, indeed, have subdivisions. Cutter defended these subdivisions as necessary for arranging long files of entries under a subject heading, and Haykin tried, as far as possible, to limit subdivision to form, place, and time. However, Haykin's examples only underline the question left unanswered by Cutter: If the original subject heading can be subdivided, is it *truly* the direct and specific heading for the books listed under it?

Subdivision: Persons and Places

Thus far we have talked of subdivision in general. There are several special problems. The dictionary catalog, wrote Cutter, is distinguished by "its individual entry . . . The alphabetico-classed catalog enters a life of Napoleon and a history of England under *Biography* and *History*; the dictionary enters them under *Napoleon* and *England*. This is the invariable and chief distinction between the two" (p.19). Access to the name of a person or the name of a place is, indeed, often direct. But in practice the name of that person or place may itself stand at the head of several subdivisions. Sometimes the name itself is a subdivision.

Persons

Some of Haykin's examples of headings for persons follow:

Shakespeare, William—Biography—Ancestry.
                          —Last Years.
                —Forgeries—Collier.
Napoleon I—Elba and the Hundred Days, 1814–1815—Drama.
Shakespeare in fiction, drama, poetry, etc.
Goethe as theater director.

Of these six headings only the last two are direct and specific headings, and they are exceptions to the general practice exemplified in the first four (which are alphabetico-classed). These two exceptions are defended not because they are direct and specific headings, but because subdivision might give us:

Shakespeare, William—Poetry.
Goethe, Johann Wolfgang von—As theater director.

The first, we are told, could be taken to apply to Shakespeare's own poetry instead of to Shakespeare as the subject of poetry. The second has a subdivision which would be inappropriately filed with subheadings such as *Anniversaries*. Use of the brief form of the person's name in the approved phrase headings requires, of course, reference from the full form of the name. Finally, it may be worth noting that the name of a person (Collier) and the name of a place (Elba) appear as subheadings in these examples.

Places

On choice between subject and place for a heading, Cutter offered no one answer. In Rule 164 he says that "the only satisfactory method is double entry . . . to put, for instance, a work on the geology of California under both *California* and *Geology*," but because this would make the catalog "very long, we are generally obliged to choose between country and scientific subject."

His very next rule (No.165) tells us to enter under place. Under Rule 343 (discussed above p.72) he has a long list of possible subject subheadings under the name of a country. He then remarks (p.127) that "former usage" allowed only such things as history, travel, and description under a country's name, while such things as that country's art, literature, and botany were put with the general works on these subjects. "But the tendency of the dictionary catalog is towards national classification; that is, in separating what relates to the parts of a subject, as is required by its *specific* principle, it necessarily brings together all that relates to a country in every aspect, as it would what relates to any other individual."

Elsewhere (p.75), when discussing the compound subject heading, he has urged that if the adjective in the phrase "implies the name of a place, as in *French literature*," it is "most convenient" to make the subject a subdivision under the name of the country. "It is not of the slightest importance that this introduces the *appearance* of an alphabetico-classed catalog, so long as the main object of a dictionary, ready reference, is attained."

This would seem to indicate that the "specific principle" abolishes the alphabetico-classed subject heading, which begins with the name of a subject, and creates the alphabetico-classed subject heading, which begins with the name of a place. In practice LC has used subdivision sometimes by place, sometimes by subject. Haykin remarks only that "the basis for subdivision of some subjects *by* place and the use of other subjects as subdivisions *under* names of places is not likely to be clear to the reader," and he urges liberal use of cross references (p.32).

Bartol Brinkler in 1962 declared that LC practice as shown in the LC list of subject headings was "quite chaotic" (*Library Resources and Technical Services*, 6:59 [1962]). Like Cutter, he suggested duplicate entry but decided it would swell the catalog too much. Failing this, he urged "reestablishment of a definite and consistent policy."

In the LC comment on Brinkler's article (*Library Resources and Technical Services*, 6:63–64 [1962]), John Cronin remarked that "subject headings are divided by place or place by subject in accordance with the presumed primary interest of the readers." This means subdivision of place by subject for "subjects whose predominant interest is focused on the area, i.e., in the fields of history, geography, and government." But if "the subject is primarily of interest to the subject specialist, subdivision of subject by place is applied, i.e., in the natural sciences, technology, and law." In other areas such as the social sciences "the cataloger must decide whether the subject or the area are of predominant interest to the reader . . . In case of doubt, subject divided by place will be favored. In the last analysis, however, the choice between the two often depends on the cataloger's subjective judgment which may be tempered by his knowledge of the objectives of his particular catalog and the clientele it is to serve." In practice, then, LC like Cutter offers no one definite answer, but, unlike Cutter, LC has swung away from a general preference for entry under place.

One quite special aspect of place headings may be worth noting. Haykin suggests the headings *Volga River* and *English Channel* but *Dover, Strait of* and *Mexico, Gulf of* (p.49). This is simply another instance of the problem of the phrase heading and possible inversion to bring first what is considered the more important part of the phrase.

Subdivision: Duplicate Entry

We have noted above (p.77) that Cutter and Brinkler suggested duplicate entry as a possible solution between place and subject entry, but rejected it as probably too greatly increasing the bulk of the catalog. Haykin does suggest (p.57–60) that sometimes duplicate entry "can be justified on the grounds that it meets the equal needs of two groups of readers." Some of his examples follow (the numbering is my own):

1. U.S.—Foreign relations—France.
   France—Foreign relations—U.S.
2. Literature, Comparative—English and German.
   Literature, Comparative—German and English.
3. English literature—Translations from Chinese.
   Chinese literature—Translations into English.
4. Irish literature (English).
   English literature—Irish authors.
5. Gnatcatchers.
   Birds—California.
6. Tapeworms.
   Parasites—Man.

Miss Pettee has some other examples (p.69–71):

7. Church and state in Norway.
   Norway—Church history.
8. Buddha and Buddhism—Japan.
   Japan—Religion.
9. For a book on the Battle of Waterloo:
   Waterloo, Battle of, 1815.
   Napoleon I—Elba and the hundred days.
10. For a book on the cults of Lesbos:
    Lesbos.
    Cultus, Greek.
    Mythology, Greek.

With No.1, 2, and 4, duplicate entry could be eliminated by the use in each case of a cross reference from one form to the other. With

No.1 and perhaps with No.2 it might be desirable to keep both headings but use them as different headings for different sets of books depending on the point of view of authors involved. With No.10 we have duplicate entry for place and subject, and none of the headings is direct and specific.

With each of the others (No.5, 6, 7, 8, and 9) there is a direct and specific heading and also a heading for the broader subject which includes the specific subject. Miss Pettee defends the practice because "it borrows the advantages of the classed catalog." In No.10, for example, "if all the special cults are given a second entry under the general heading, Cultus, Greek, we have a very useful file, easy to consult. These small topics, such as Hades, Zeus, Delphic oracles, Athena, etc., scattered through the catalog require a tedious search by the student anxious to collect them." Of No.7, if the library has few books on the church history of Norway and this particular book is the best, she asks "Why not give it the extra heading, Norway—Church history?"

Yet Cutter, although not himself always consistent in the matter, had answered the "why not?" At the close of his discussion of the "specific entry rule" (No.161), Cutter wrote: "On the other hand, difficulty arises from the public, or a part of it, being accustomed to think of certain subjects in connection with their including classes . . . so that there is a temptation to enter books doubly, once under the specific heading to satisfy the rule, and once under the class to satisfy the public. The dictionary principle does not forbid this. If room can be spared, the cataloger may put what he pleases under an extensive subject (a class), provided he puts the less comprehensive works also under their respective specific headings. The objection to this is that, if all the specifics are thus entered, the bulk of the catalog is enormously increased; and that, if a selection is made, it must depend entirely upon the 'judgment' i.e., the prepossessions and accidental associations of the cataloger, and there will be an end to all uniformity, and probably the public will not be better satisfied, not understanding why they do not find class-entry in all cases."

The Third Objective

"The public, or a part of it," wrote Cutter, is "accustomed to thinking of certain subjects in connection with their including classes" (see above).

There are, indeed, two problems not directly dealt with in Cutter's "Objects," perhaps because they relate not to books but to subjects themselves: (1) The specific subject of a book is a unity in itself, but (2) The specific subject of that book is also part of a broader subject which may itself be the specific subject matter of another book. This means that if the catalog is to answer Cutter's second objective ("To show what the library has on a given subject"), it must have a third objective: To show what books the library has on broader subjects which include the narrow topic the user specifically wants. In short, specific entry cannot escape classification.

Cutter's answer to this third objective was his "syndetic approach." Rules 187 and 188: "Make references from general subjects to their various subordinate subjects and also to coordinate and illustrative subjects [and] make references occasionally from specific [i.e., narrow] subjects to general subjects." (See p.66 above, No.5.)

To Cutter, perhaps, this third objective was not too important. The dictionary catalog, he wrote, having attained its object—"facility of reference—is at liberty to try to secure some of the advantages of classification and system in its own way." The dictionary catalog's subject entries, "individual, general, limited, extensive, thrown together without any logical arrangement, in most absurd proximity—*Abscess* followed by *Absenteeism* and that by *Absolution, Clubfoot* next to *Clubs* . . . are a mass of utterly disconnected particles . . . But by a well-devised net-work of cross-references the mob becomes an army . . ." (p.79).

How good an army?

Cutter suggested that in "Full" cataloging there would be references not only from subjects to all their parts but also "from Classes of persons (Merchants, Lawyers, Artists, Quakers, etc.) to individuals belonging to those classes; from Cities to persons connected with them . . . from Countries to their colonies, provinces, counties, cities, etc. . . . from *History* to rulers and statesmen . . . from *Literature* to authors . . . *Art* to artists." Other catalogs "will make [only] such of these references as seem most likely to be useful" (p.79). At this point the "army" begins to straggle.

Haykin (p.14) limits the syndetic approach to "see also" references, and (p.15) he distinguishes between:

1. Specific references—"see also" references directed to particular headings—and
2. General references—"see also" references to a class:

    Birds.
    See also names of different kinds of birds, e.g., Humming birds; Plovers; Terns.

As to the possibility that general references defeat the syndetic aspect, he urges that probably few readers would want all the material in the library to which specific references would lead and that they would do better to use bibliographies or systematic treatises.

Haykin (p.16) does, like Cutter, endorse reference from classes to individuals:

Economists, American
> *see also*

Veblen, Thorstein, 1857–1929
Walker, Francis Amasa, 1840–1897

and:

Epic poetry
> *see also*

Chanson de Roland
Kalevala
Nibelungenlied

These—and indeed all—"see also" references are costly and awkward to apply, and they are not as obviously useful as "see" references. In practice, catalogers have tended to follow only one small part of Cutter's directive about the third objective: "Make such of these references as seem most likely to be useful" (see p.80 above).

Thus far we have dealt only with those references which lead "down"—from general topics to narrower topics. What of the references which lead "up"—from a subject to a more general subject which contains it? This is probably more important to the third objective: To show what books the library has on broader subjects which include the narrow topic the user specifically wants. Here we find a curious thing: Cutter called for such references only "occasionally" (Rule 188), and Haykin does not call for them at all. Cutter admitted the need: "The very best description of a single plant or of a family of plants may perhaps be contained in a botanical encyclopaedia" and "this fact must be impressed upon the inquirer in the preface of the [printed] catalog or in a printed card"; but "it is out of the question to make all possible references of the ascending kind."

The "army" is routed before the fight begins. Perhaps it is just as well. If the system of "see also" references were complete both going up and coming down, it is likely that the user would never bother to follow the directions hither and yon. Even if he did bother, he would soon grow weary.

Cutter and Haykin: Summary

We often talk as though by "specific" we mean a "narrow" subject. Actually we mean only the specific subject of a particular book or group of books; this specific subject may be "narrow" or "broad." And we mean an entry without any classification device, an entry to be found directly under the subject's own name in an alphabetical catalog. That is, we mean direct and specific entry.

But in practice the subject heading produced by this principle of direct and specific entry is sometimes not direct. It may require further subdivision (i.e., classification) by time, place, form—sometimes even by subject—before it brings us to the specific subject of a particular book or group of books. Nor is the heading always specific. It may instead be a heading for the class of which the book's specific subject is only a part if (1) there is not yet an accepted name for the book's specific subject, or (2) the library has only a few or no books on any subject within that class, or (3) the cataloger makes duplicate entry, one for the specific subject of a book and one for the class of which that subject is part.

There are two objectives of subject entry:

1. To enable a person to find a book of which the subject is known.
2. To show what the library has on a given subject.

Because of the nature of subjects, there is a third objective if we are to serve completely the second:

3. To show what books the library has on broader subjects which include the subject the user specifically wants.

How well does the direct and specific subject heading serve these three objectives? To serve the first objective, the heading need be only specific. To serve the second objective (as long as we talk only of the subjects of entire books), the heading need be only specific and uniform. But a heading can serve the third objective only if it has some sort of classification device, e.g., the alphabetico-classed heading. The direct and specific heading cannot serve the third objective at all. If we use the direct and specific heading, we need also a network of "see also" references leading "up" and "down" and "across" from one heading to another. Librarians have found such a network an intolerable burden; it seems possible that the user also would find it such.

What are we to do? There are several alternatives to Cutter. We shall consider three: (1) the Subject Heading List, (2) the Alphabetico-Classed Catalog, and (3) the Noun Approach.

The Subject Heading List

Catalogers have two devices by which they strive to be consistent: rules and records of how they have applied the rules. Broadly speaking, to the extent that rules fail to guide by themselves, records flourish. A library can, for instance, maintain an authority file for subject headings and cross references used, and the cataloger needs only to consult this file to keep his work consistent. An individual file is rather expensive, and it may differ from the authority in other libraries. Early the idea of a published list developed. Such a list promotes uniformity among libraries, gives the cataloger ideas about the phrasing of subject headings new to him, and can (if the library wishes to do so) be used as an authority file simply by entering checks opposite headings used.

In 1895 the first published list appeared, the work of an ALA committee. This ALA list went through three editions and then gave way to the LC list and the Sears list. The ALA list and the Sears list are largely compilations of the practice in a number of medium-sized libraries, and the LC list simply records LC practice. Broadly speaking, the LC list provides headings for narrower subjects; therefore, it results in headings which often are more specific. The ALA list and Sears list, on the other hand, followed Cutter's idea (see p.72 above) that in a small collection broader headings might often be better.

In addition to the general lists, there have been many special lists, perhaps well over a hundred, ranging from lists attempting to meet the needs of a special kind of user—e.g., children—to those attempting to meet the needs of a special subject collection—e.g., a music library. It is sometimes urged that the special list for children is necessary because of vocabulary; yet it may be desirable that children become familiar with the same words they will need later in a Sears- or LC-based set of subject headings. (We do not, for instance, construct special piano keyboards to take care of the small hands of the child.) The list for a special collection is another matter; Haykin notes, for instance (p.73), that in a chemistry library *Laboratory manuals* would be better than *Chemistry—Laboratory manuals, Elements* than *Chemical elements.*

The subject heading list poses at least three problems:

1. The list must be kept up to date. This, of course, would be true even if the library were simply following a subject heading code; but in that case the library would adopt its own new headings. If the LC list or any other list is the standard for a library, then local changes and additions are always made in fear that the next supplement or edition of the list will use a different word or phrase for the new subject. If it is different, the cataloger will have to change cards already made or record the library's practice in the printed list so that headings will be consistent.

2. The subject heading list admits the failure of the rules. This admission discourages further experimentation with the basic philosophy of the rules. Instead, we tinker with the headings themselves, turning

each in whatever direction seems best at the time. The lists just grow.

3. Moreover, the published list freezes practice, particularly if the list's headings appear on printed cards such as those of LC or Wilson. Over the years these cards build up in the library a big investment in the status quo of subject heading work. It would be costly to change basic philosophy; it is much easier to rationalize practice, as Haykin and Julia Pettee did.

Yet Cutter, from whom we get this practice, wanted not merely "to set forth the rules in a systematic way," he wanted also "to investigate what might be called the first principles of cataloging" (p.3). In slavishly following Cutter on subject headings, we pay him little heed.

The Alphabetico-Classed Catalog

Perhaps the best-known alphabetico-classed catalog was that prepared at Harvard under the supervision of Ezra Abbot, beginning in 1861. There were about five hundred major subject divisions. The entire catalog was arranged alphabetically by these major divisions, by subdivisions under each division, by sub-subdivisions under each subdivision, and so on. This "Index of Subjects" was one catalog; the "Index of Authors" was another (Ranz, p.70; Pettee, p.39). A number of libraries adopted the alphabetico-classed catalog for a while.

There were at least two problems:

1. Should a particular subject be treated independently or as a subdivision? Cutter remarks (p.19) that Abbot had such specific headings as *Ink, Jute, Leather, Life-savers, Locks, Mortars, Perfumery, Safes, Salt, Smoke, Snow, Varnish, Vitriol.* How would the user know whether to look for such a topic under its individual name or under the name of some class which included it?

2. How could awkwardness be avoided? The Harvard catalog with its elaborate headings became so cumbersome that by 1886 it was necessary to print a detailed topical index, and some years later the catalog was turned into a dictionary catalog.

Cutter, who had been Abbot's assistant, thought highly of the alphabetico-classed catalog for several years, even after he had developed the dictionary catalog at the Boston Athenaeum. In his *Rules* he indicated that there was very little difference between the convenience of the two systems for a person who understands both (Ranz, p.72). The alphabetico-classed system was best "for the thorough investigation of comprehensive subjects; the dictionary system for finding quickly what relates to a person, a place, or other special topic" (Cutter in *Public Libraries*, p.540). On the other hand, the alphabetico-classed subject heading is, perhaps, the only subject heading which attempts alone to serve all of the three objectives.

From time to time the shortcomings of the direct and specific heading have brought us back toward the theory of the alphabetico-classed. In 1909, for instance, J. C. M. Hanson remarked that there was "undeniably a strong tendency in the Library of Congress catalog to bring related subjects together by means of inversion of headings, by combinations of two or more subject-words, and even by subordination of one subject to another. Yes, the tendency at times is so noticeable that it may seem as if an effort were being made to establish a compromise between the dictionary and the alphabetico-classed catalog, just as the latter was intended as a compromise between the systematic and the alphabetic plans of arrangement." Hanson suggested two reasons for this "tendency": (1) Use of the LC catalog would be "more and more" by the "student and the investigator, and they are best served by having related topics brought together so far as can be accomplished without a too serious violation of the dictionary principle." (2) Strict adherence "to the principle of specific entry under minute subjects to be arranged in regular order of their names" would cause the catalog to "resolve itself in course of time into a mere subject index in which it becomes practically impossible to guard against the ultimate dispersion of the literature on one and the same topic under various headings." Hanson cited as an example of LC practice at that time the following series of headings and references:

Eastern question
  (to be used for "general works")
Eastern question—Balkan
  (with cross references from *Balkan question* and from *Near Eastern question*)
Eastern question—Central Asia
  (with cross references from *Middle Eastern question, Central Asian question,* and *Anglo-Russian question*)
Eastern question—Far East
  (with cross references from *Far Eastern question, East Asian question, Chino-Japanese question, Pacific-Asian question*)

"Hundreds of similar illustrations," he noted, "could be enumerated where, by inversion or subordination, a specific subject has been made to stand with the general topic to which it bears relation" (American Library Association, *Papers and Proceedings of the Meeting at Bretton Woods* [1909] p.389–90). Later LC practice moved toward stricter use of the direct and specific heading, but some remnants of Hanson's "hundreds of similar illustrations" still survived in the LC lists of subject headings, e.g., "Milk substitutes see Food substitutes."

In a thought-provoking article, "How Specific Is Specific?" (*Journal of Cataloging and Classification,* 11:3–8 [1955]), Oliver L. Lilley pointed out that "specificity" means different things in different subject areas, in different kinds of libraries, in different books, and in the different needs of people—or even to the same person at two different times. "The reader will be disappointed who is optimistic enough to expect to find a book on 'How to patch men's pants,' and who tries the 'specific' headings *Patching; Men;* or *Pants*." When we tell the user to look for the specific heading we are in effect "inviting him to close his eyes and 'pick a word' . . . If he's lucky and picks the same word we are thinking of, he wins the game . . ."

Perhaps half in jest, Lilley then suggested that we "turn over a new leaf" and say to the reader that "there are just 500 possible words you need to consider before you begin, and all of these are printed on a chart" at the catalog. "Select the word that stands for the *group* or *class* of things to which your topic belongs, look under that word . . . and you will be led by . . . understandable subdivisions to the exact heading we use for the material you want."

This is, of course, the theory of the alphabetico-classed catalog, and Lilley, like Abbot, began with five hundred major subject divisions. Yet, the word or phrase at the end of the line following each of these terms is (as we have noted above) a "specific" word or phrase, and as such it is subject to all of the problems of "specificity." If, for instance, we agree with Lilley and Cutter that different kinds of libraries have different levels of "specificity," how will the user know that in one library he will find L. C. Wroth's *Colonial Printer* (see Lilley, p.4–5) under a subject heading's last word *Printing,* that in another library the line stops with *Printing—History,* while in a third it stops with *Printing—History—U.S.*?

Perhaps more important, where will this user find the book on "How to patch men's pants"? Under an end-of-the-line word *Patching,* or *Men* or *Pants*? In fact, of course, the "specific subject" of this book is "How to patch men's pants." Will *that* be the end of one of the five hundred lines? We return to a question raised (or at least implied) earlier (p.67): What is a "specific subject"? Is it always a topic at the end of a line of topics? Or is it sometimes that topic combined with one or more topics at the end of one or more other lines of topics?

The advantage of the direct and specific heading is not simply its boasted direct alphabetic access to a specific topic; even more important may be its ability to combine topics from different areas. Perhaps there will never be a direct and specific heading *How to patch men's pants.* Cutter did offer such headings as *Flower fertilization, Ancients and Moderns, Paterna paternis materna maternis*; and Haykin, *Agri-*

cultural credit, Literature and morals, Divine right of kings. Cutter's compound heading, with all its defects (see p.70 above), recognized the complex nature of many subjects.

The Noun Approach (Schwartz and Cutter)

In defending his somewhat haphazard rule (No.175) for the compound heading and its occasional inversion (see p.71 above), Cutter felt it necessary to build an elaborate answer to a proposal by Jacob Schwartz. For a noun preceded by an adjective Schwartz would:

1. If possible, reduce the phrase to its equivalent noun—e.g., *Moral philosophy* to *Ethics* or to *Morals*; *Sanitary science* to *Hygiene*; *Social science* to *Sociology*.

2. If such reduction is impossible, invert the words with the noun first—e.g., *Chemistry, Agriculture; Anatomy, Comparative; History, Ancient.*

To this proposal Cutter had several objections (the numbering is mine):

1. It would put "a great many subjects" where nobody would expect to find them, e.g.:

"works on the	would hardly be looked for under
Alimentary canal	Canal
Dangerous classes	Classes
Digestive organs	Organs"

He continued the list to include fourteen terms.

2. "In most cases the noun expresses a class, the adjective . . . makes the name that of a subclass (as International law, Remittent disease . . .) and to adopt the noun (the class) as the heading is to violate the fundamental principle of the dictionary catalog."

3. Schwartz had urged that the noun approach would be "more easily grasped by the common mind" and that it was "precisely analogous" to entry of names of persons; e.g., he suggested that

Smith, John
Smith, Joseph
Smith, William

follow the same principle as

History, Ancient
History, Ecclesiastical
History, Modern

All this, said Cutter, was "plausible" if the public could get accustomed to it, but "it might be difficult to teach the rule." Everyone knows the practice with personal names because it is in all catalogs, but in a catalog of fifty thousand names of persons, there would be less than three hundred noun-adjective headings; "the use of the rule would be so infrequent that it would not remain in the memory."

4. Logic will not bother the user. If he wants *Comparative anatomy*, he finds it "where he first looks, under *C*." He does not care where *Morbid anatomy* is, and if another man looks for it under *M*, he is easily referred to *Anatomy, Morbid* "and does not stop to notice that *Comparative anatomy* is not there." On the other hand, the user "taking a general survey of all that the library possesses on anatomy" would probably "be too intent" on his project to "criticize the arrangement, provided the reference from *Anatomy* to *Comparative anatomy* were perfectly clear."

5. The reader must learn the specific-entry rule if he is to use the dictionary catalog with ease; no need to burden him with learning an exception to the rule "which the noun rule certainly is."

To Cutter's objections we may perhaps say: No.1 is, of course, correct, although it may be that in some cases an entirely different phrase might be used. No.2, if carried to its logical conclusion, would forbid any inverted adjective-noun headings. No.3 is probably correct if Cutter's statistics are correct. No.4 is sheer supposition, and in practice the cross-reference system in many catalogs leaves much to be desired. No.5 is true; yet on the following page (p.75) he says of his proposed headings such as *France—Literature, Greece—Art*: "It is not of the slightest importance that this introduces the appearance of an alphabetico-classed catalog, so long as the main object of a dictionary, ready reference, is attained."

This last statement brings us to Marie Louise Prevost.

The Noun Approach (Prevost)

In 1946, Marie Louise Prevost appealed from Cutter to Schwartz (*Library Quarterly* 16:140–51 [1946]). She assailed Cutter's concern about the "public." "What is the public . . . ? Children, young people, adults; the expert, the inept, the illiterate, the savant; scientists, artists, authors, teachers, and—librarians." It is a "patent absurdity to speak of cataloging according to the 'public mind' as if that mind were a single entity."

Subject heading lists have just grown, and none is a "logically thought out product." We must "cast loose all ties with the past . . . analyze our objectives and our practices . . . and then reconstitute . . . Our aim must be to make of [the] catalog a simpler tool for the librarian and, with a modicum of initiation, for the intelligent reader. The less intelligent must lean on professional competence—as, in fact, they always have done."

Miss Prevost retold the story of Cutter's debate with Schwartz and called on us to return to Schwartz and expand his rule. *Her* basic rule would be: "All headings begin with the noun indicating the direct subject." The adjectival approach scatters aspects of a subject "to the four winds or, literally, to the twenty-six letters . . . the noun-plus-subhead keeps an entire subject segregated and intact. At present we have columns of headings in which 'School' is used as an adjective, then 'Schools' with numerous subheads, and then about two dozen types of schools beginning with as many different adjectives. Who is to know, offhand, that 'Attendance' is to be found under 'School,' 'Accounting' under 'Schools,' and 'Art' under 'Art' but not under 'Schools' at all?" Instead, she would have:

Schools—Accounting
Schools—Art
Schools—Attendance
Schools—Commercial

"with no long list of *see also* references and no further, usually incomplete, list of references from inversions."

So much for the adjectival heading; for other compound headings she endorsed the idea of an unfiled word or words within parentheses:

Salesmanship—(to) Children
Accounting—(for the) Executive
Education—(relation to) Democracy
Railroads—(regulation by) Government
World war, 1939–45—Peace—(affected by) Democracy
World war, 1939–45—Peace—(effect on) Religion.

For the last two there would be duplicate entry:

Democracy—(effect on) World war, 1939–45—Peace
Religion—(affected by) World war, 1939–45—Peace.

The World War entries illustrate her principle that we should "enter under both 'keys' with appropriate subheads, when two key headings (headings having, or fitted to have, subheads) meet in a subject term, never permitting the substitution of a *see reference* for either" (p.145). Also she would enter names of events, including wars, invariably under name of event, with *see also* to history plus dates, as desired.

Miss Prevost gave four "general rules" (p.149):

1. Be specific, but via the subhead, not the adjective.
2. Be definitive. Vague and ambiguous headings should be either eliminated, delimited by clear definition, or replaced by two or more concrete headings (as for the "ands").
3. Inverted titles are not to be used as substitutes for headings . . .

4. Subject takes precedence of place invariably. Where subject subheads under place are desired, as for local needs, make the reverse
entry also. [She would allow place plus subhead "History" plus
dates.]

Schwartz (see p.87 above) had urged that his system would be
easier for the "common mind" because it was "precisely analogous"
to entry of names of persons, and Cutter had countered that in a
catalog of fifty thousand personal names there would be less than
three hundred noun-adjective headings and that the use of Schwartz's
rule would be "so infrequent that it would not remain in the memory." Miss Prevost, however, would apply the Schwartz rule to *all*
headings now treated as compound headings. This would greatly extend the use of the rule; perhaps it would now be frequent enough
that it *would* remain in the memory.

Some of her noun headings have caused eyebrows to rise. She suggested (p.145) that *Iron trade* would become *Iron—Trade* but *Iron
age* would be *Age—Iron* and *Intercultural relations* would become
Cultures—Interrelation (or possibly *Race—Interrelations*). All headings beginning with "Natural" or "Nature" would be recast into a
single alphabet or subheadings under *Nature* (p.147). *International
relations* would become *Nations—Interrelations*, and *International law*
would become *Nations—Law* and *Law—International*.

Perhaps the most serious objection has been that originally raised
by Cutter about Schwartz's proposal: The idea of noun entry violates
the specific-entry rule (see p.88 above). Allied to this objection is
the feeling that the Prevost approach is a form of the alphabetico-
classed catalog (cf. Jolley, p.117-18).

As to "specific entry," Miss Prevost's first rule (see p.89 above) required specificity. The only difference between it and Cutter is the
means by which specificity is gained. Of course, many headings in our
catalogs today are not specific by anybody's definition, and many of
them, indeed, are alphabetico-classed—at least as much so in appearance as those proposed by Miss Prevost. But there is a major difference:
The true alphabetico-classed catalog, such as that of Abbot and that
proposed by Lilley, uses only some five hundred *basic* terms; every
heading is then a subdivision somewhere along the line under one of
those terms. What Miss Prevost proposed, however, was not some
universal classification scheme with every heading based on a main
class. Instead, she wanted only what she said: "Be specific, but via the
subhead."

Perhaps we have made opposition to the alphabetico-classed catalog an article of faith. Perhaps the answer to our subject heading
problem—if it comes—will not be doctrinal.

The Noun Approach (Others)

Speaking broadly, the major problem with direct and specific entry is that posed by the arrangement of the elements in the compound heading. We have examined in some detail the elaborate headings of Cutter and Haykin which attempt to use—so far as possible—natural language arrangement. The alternative is to break up the elements of the heading; this we have found in the alphabetico-classed catalog and in the noun approach of Schwartz and Miss Prevost. Each of these has dealt with the American general catalog. Other ideas have been put forth, intended to meet the needs of the libraries of another country and/or a particular kind of library. We shall look briefly at some of them.

In his *Systematic Indexing* (1911), J. O. Kaiser, concerned primarily with the problem of the special library, suggested that subjects could be arranged each as a "concrete" followed by a "process." A concrete is a thing, a place, or an abstract term which does not indicate a process. A process is basically something done to a concrete: a description, a method of treating the concrete, an aspect or modification of the concrete, and so on. Concretes are main headings; processes are subheadings. This might produce today such headings as:

Wool—Scouring
Land—Cultivation (instead of the simple heading Agriculture)
Books—Description (instead of the simple heading Bibliography)
Paint—Application

Such a system might achieve consistency, but now and then at the expense of seeming too arbitrary (as with Agriculture and Bibliography above).

S. R. Ranganathan offers (instead of only two) five categories of terms arranged broadly in the following sequence: Energy/Matter/Personality/Space/Time. (This is, of course, a rearrangement of the categories in his Colon scheme, to be discussed in Chapter 6.) In the subject heading *Harvesting—Grapes*, "Energy" is Harvesting and "Personality" is Grapes. (See Coates, p.43–45.) Probably there should be more than Kaiser's two categories of terms to determine sequence, but they should be categories more easily defined than "Personality."

J. E. L. Farradane distinguishes terms not by categories but by the relationships between them. His scheme provides nine kinds of relationships which determine the way in which terms may be placed together. For each relationship there is a sign consisting of two parts; the order of the parts shows the direction of the relationship. For example, in the phrase "signing a will in the presence of witnesses," signing has an "action" relationship, witnesses a "co-presence" relationship. The signs for these relationships are:

/– is the object of action by
ø in the presence of

So, expressed in notation, the heading would be:

Will /– Signing ø Witnesses

The order of the elements can be reversed if required, but the signs must then also be in reversed form:

Witnesses ø Signing –/ Will

This ingenious scheme may be too complicated for general use; moreover, as shown in the example, it does not determine the first word in the sequence. Finally, it may be that some people will suggest more than nine possible relationships. (See Farradane in *Sayers Memorial Volume* [1961], p.120–55, and Coates, p.45–49.)

E. J. Coates draws a line between "term significance" and "term relationships" (p.50 ff.). The most significant term, he suggests, is that "which evokes the clearest mental image." In the phrase "springing of cats" we can visualize a cat, but "if we remove the cat, leaving only the term 'springing' what is there left to imagine? Perhaps only the vague trajectory of anything that rises from the ground and then falls, a curving line in fact." Broadly speaking, a term which calls up a static image—e.g., cat—is thus more significant than one which denotes actions or processes. A static image may be a "material" or a "thing," and in the mind's eye a "thing" has a boundary, a "material" does not. The name of a thing is, therefore, a more significant term. So for the basic sequence of "term significance," Coates suggests:

Thing/Material/Action.

Suppose that one has two or more equally concrete terms and that in reversed order they mean different things, e.g., *Conveyor belt* and *Belt conveyor*? "Term relationship" is both important and difficult. Prepositions express the simpler relationships between concepts, and yet they bring out the differences. Thus *Conveyor belt* and *Belt conveyor* become "Belt of conveyor" and "Conveyor with belt" respectively.

Working along this line, Coates develops a "Relationship Table" (opposite p.55) in which he sets forth in columns the relationships of twenty different types of compound. For each type of compound there are entries under five columns. Entries for the first type are described below. (Entries themselves are in italics.)

Col. 1: Type of compound—*Action on Thing*
Col. 2: Subject Heading Order—*Thing, Action*
Col. 3: Subject Heading agrees or reverses significance order—
Agrees
Col. 4: Subject Heading agrees or reverses amplified phrase or-
der—*Reverses*
Col. 5: Usual relationship words in amplified phrase—*of*

Two examples of this relationship with the resulting subject headings
are:

1. Phrase: Pile driving
   Amplified phrase: Driving of piles
   Subject heading: *Piles—Driving*
2. Phrase: Village planning
   Amplified phrase: Planning of villages
   Subject heading: *Villages—Planning*

This is a rather intricate business, and, of course, there is always
the chance that at least one "relationship" has been overlooked in the
table. Moreover, there is no reason to believe that the user would
always have the same notion about the way to get a particular relationship into a subject heading. On the other hand, it seems possible
that a list of subject headings developed in line with the table would
at least grow consistently. It might even be that lists developed independently in different libraries would be similar enough to remove
the need of a general list of subject headings such as those of Sears
or LC.

Every approach we have talked of thus far has sought to bring
some sort of system to the statement of relationships between terms
in a subject consisting of more than one word. Mortimer Taube's ingenious Uniterm system of coordinate indexing ignores subject heading structure. Each subject heading is a single term, and each item
indexed receives as many terms as are necessary. Then if one wants
something on the influence of subject A on subject B, he looks at the
items which are listed under *both* A and B. He would get also any
items on the influence of subject B on subject A. This crudely brief
account of the system makes it sound cumbersome. It was intended
for scientific reports dealing with some specialized topic, not for general library catalog use.

Yet the central idea is intriguing, and Jolley (p.120) suggests that
the "concept of bibliographical coordination as a method of subject
limitation is of great importance" because "the specific subject of
books is often a collocation of two general subjects." As an example,
he cites a book on *The attitude of the Catholic Church towards witch-*

craft and the allied practices of sorcery and magic. For this book LC
has the subject headings

> Magic
> Witchcraft
> Catholic Church—History

None of these, of course, is the specific subject of the book; and Jolley
feels that the person who looks for the book by subject "will be faced
with the task of examining every entry under whichever heading he
chooses." This would be "tedious and time consuming" even in a small
library. He suggests instead the two headings

> Catholic Church—Magic
> Magic—Catholic Church

which he feels would "lead directly to the specific subject," although
"admittedly these headings are ambiguous." To make them more definite, he suggests the use of prepositional words or phrases within
parentheses as Miss Prevost's system allows. Without the Prevost device it seems not impossible that to look at all the cards under one
of Jolley's two headings might be as "tedious and time consuming"
as to use the LC headings.

Thus we come full circle. The problem for us, as it was for Cutter,
is the compound heading. Anyone can handle a single-word heading.
But we want something more tangible than Cutter's "usage" or "convenience of the public" to bring consistent and orderly handling of
the compound heading. From Schwartz to Taube—and beyond—the
noun approach has seemed to be the key.

The Non-Subject Heading

In Chapter 3, on author and title entry and heading, we examined
a creation of catalogers' convention: the non-author heading (p.40).
Catalogers' convention has also created the non-subject heading. Such
a heading looks like a subject heading, but it brings together books
by some characteristic other than subject. Further, it is conventional
for catalogers to call these non-subject headings "Assembling Headings," although, of course, any kind of heading (author, title, or subject) "assembles" books to which that heading applies. Perhaps the
most common non-subject heading, like a quite common non-author
heading (p.43), is a heading for form.

Cutter's Rule 189 called for a "form entry for collections of works
in any form of literature"—e.g., *Poetry, Drama, Fiction, English drama,
English fiction.* This rule, he pointed out, "confines itself to collections," although "it would be convenient to have full lists of the single
works in the library in all the various kinds of literature . . . when

space can be afforded." He called also for form entries for single
works in the "rarer literatures, as Japanese, or Kalmuc, or Cherokee"
(Rule 190); for encyclopedias, indexes, and the like (Rule 191); and
for periodicals (Rule 192). Since Cutter, however, we have generally
tended to agree with Miss Pettee that such headings "should be considered exceptions, not the rule" (Pettee, p.145).

As with author headings, so with subject headings, generally form
is not an independent heading but simply a subdivision (see p.43).
Thus we may combine a true author heading with a form division—
e.g., *U.S. Laws, statutes, etc.* Or we may combine a true subject heading with a form division—e.g., *Agriculture—Periodicals.*

The other non-author headings for main entry noted above (p.41)
were the pseudo-author heading and the institution heading. These
respectively bring together books by their subjects—e.g., the defendant in a trial—and by the geographical location of certain corporate
authors. Both are conventional; neither is logical. Logic would seem
to call for main entry of each directly under a heading for the name
of the author. The pseudo-author heading might then give way to a
true subject heading. And if we wanted to assemble corporate authors
by location, we might do it with a non-subject heading—e.g., *New
York (City)—Churches—Protestant Episcopal—St. George's. Washington—Hospitals—St. Agnes.* This might also be more useful because it
would assemble under each location all institutions of a certain type,
e.g., hospitals.

What Is the Book About?

We often want a book on This-and-That rather than a book by
So-and-So. Cutter gave us catalog entry under the direct and specific
heading for the subject of the book. But this heading asks at least
three questions: (1) What if the book's subject has no one readily
accepted name? (2) What if the subject's name consists of more than
one word or more than one concept? (3) What about books on broader
subjects which include the subject of the book in hand? We have yet
to answer these questions.

"No catalogue can exhibit all possible connections of thought.
Enough if it exhibit the most common, and give some clew for tracing
the rarer ones. Those that claim perfection for any system show that
they have no idea of the difficulties to be overcome"—Cutter in *Public
Libraries,* p.541.

What is the book about? What indeed?

6

Where Does It Go?
Call Numbers

Author and title headings, description, and subject headings determine the location of the entries for books in the catalog. Call numbers determine the location of the books themselves on the shelves. Part or all of a call number may be derived from a library classification scheme. For this reason the cataloger U.S.A. tends to think of and evaluate a classification scheme in terms of the book-locating efficiency of the call numbers derived from it.

The Two Objectives

Call numbers, like author and title headings, subject headings, and description, have two objectives:

1. To help the user find a book whose call number he knows, and
2. To help the user find all books of a kind together.

These two objectives, like the other pairs of objectives, look at the book as an individual and as part of a group.

Part of what *kind* of group? There are several possible arrangements of books depending on what kinds of books we want our call numbers to bring together. We may arrange books by:

1. Accession order
2. Size
3. Subject or form
4. Author
5. Date of publication
6. Combination of two or more of the above (and perhaps other) sequences.

The grouping the cataloger chooses depends also on whether he wants the books to have fixed location or relative location.

Fixed Location

Fixed location is probably older than any other system. It was popular for many centuries, and it can be found today in American libraries under certain conditions. Any of several of the arrangements listed above may appear in books with fixed location. For instance, a particular bookcase can be given to a subject, its shelves can be arranged for different sizes, and on each shelf the order can be that of accession. Or size can be first, then subject, then accession. An outstanding catalog of the fourteenth century, that of St. Martin's Priory (Dover, 1380), seems to reflect an arrangement in bookpresses represented by letters A to I. Each press represented a subject or form, except that three presses (C, D, and E) were given over to sermons and theological works, and two presses (F and G) were given to civil and canon law. Within each press the shelves were numbered, and on each shelf the books were numbered. Thus something like A.II.I would be the call number for the first book on the second shelf of Press A (Bibles and commentaries). In Charles C. Jewett's *Catalogue of the Library of Brown University* (1843), each entry is followed by two numbers in the right margin; the first refers to the shelf, the second to the position of the book upon the shelf. Addison's *Works* (1804) had call number 85 28.

The problem with fixed location is growth. Eventually even a medieval library of manuscripts ran out of shelving space and needed more bookcases. The collection could then be completely reshelved in a new sequence which included the space in both old and new cases; that is, the fixed location could be "unfixed" or, at least, "refixed." Or the old cases could be left as they were and the new cases could begin a new sequence of their own. The successive catalogs of a number of medieval libraries seem to reflect some version of one of these two devices.

Reshelving the whole collection by a new sequence preserved the second objective (all books of a kind together), but a new sequence for only the new cases violated the second objective because now books of the same kind might be found in two places. Either solution was awkward. Yet in a slowly growing medieval library of only a few hundred (or even a few thousand) volumes perhaps neither the second objective nor awkwardness mattered too much. (A modern personal library is a good example.)

Obviously there are different degrees of fixity. If a book is the sixth book on the second shelf of a specific bookcase, or if it is chained to a specific table in a specific corner of the library, this is absolute fixed location. On the other hand, if the book is the fifth book among the Bibles of folio size, then fixed location becomes merely a sequential location depending on order of acquisition. Sequential location is the next thing to relative location.

Relative Location

Gutenberg's invention was the mass production of manuscripts. After Gutenberg the problems of growth of libraries multiplied rapidly. But it was four hundred years after Gutenberg before there was a major change in shelving and call numbers. Fixed location and sequential location are awkward; but they do not pose a problem to the user as long as there is an adequate catalog and someone to get the books from the stacks for him. When there are open stacks into which the user can go and get his own books, call numbers begin to mean a lot more to him.

Fixed location does not allow us to add any new books once the presses are full, and sequential location allows new books only at the end of each sequence. But call numbers can be devised in such a way that new books can be intershelved with other books of their kind at any point on the shelves. This practice results in relative location of books, completely independent of any fixed location.

Like fixed location, relative location can use various combinations of the arrangements listed above, although users probably find subject arrangement most helpful. (Subdivision of books on a particular topic may then be by one or more of the other arrangements, e.g., by author and then by date.) Unlike fixed location, relative location thus allows for indefinite growth without having to change call numbers, and its arrangement at all times meets the second objective. The two classification schemes most used in American libraries provide call numbers which shelve books in relative location. They are the Dewey Decimal Classification and the Library of Congress Classification.

Dewey Decimal Classification (DDC)

"One Sunday during a long sermon by Pres. Stearns, while I lookt stedfastly at him without hearing a word, my mind absorbed in the vital problem, the solution flasht over me so that I jumpt in my seat and came very near shouting 'Eureka!' It was to get absolute simplicity by using the simplest known symbols, the arabic numerals as decimals with the ordinary significance of nought, to number a classification of all human knowledge in print" (quoted in Fremont Rider's *Melvil Dewey* [1944], p.28).

Thus, fifty years after the event, Melvil Dewey said the big idea had come to him. It was 1873 and he was an Amherst undergraduate library assistant not yet twenty-two. The idea had "flasht" over him, yet it had come only after long thought of the waste and inefficiency of fixed location; the idea's development was to be slow and with the help of many people.

This first and probably best known of modern classification schemes was first published three years later, in 1876. It had twelve pages of schedules setting forth knowledge in ten main classes, each subdivided decimally to make a total of one thousand classes, numbered 000 to 999; a relative index was attached. The seventeenth edition appeared in 1965 with the basic decimal plan unaltered but in two massive volumes, as compared with the modest twelve pages of 1876.

Relative location with decimals was easy. "In its simpl form a skoolboy can quikly master it . . . By mere adition of figures . . . this very simpl sistem is redily made to record the utmost refinements . . . and the Relativ Index, as simpl as a, b, c, sends the novis to the exact place where the expert has clasifyd the matter sought. Thus 942 is history of England, and 942.99055 is history of County Pembroke in Wales, under Elizabeth, 5th of the Tudors" (Dewey in DDC 17, p.64).

Now it is very easy to point out that there are probably not exactly ten main topics about which books are written, and that each of these ten topics probably does not have exactly ten subtopics, and that each subtopic probably does not have exactly ten subtopics of its own. Life is just not that simple and mechanical.

It is also very easy to point with scorn to curiosities in the scheme itself: To be caustic about the mixture of form divisions, such as Bibliography, and subject divisions, such as "Library Economy," in the General Works (000's). Or to ask why Psychology should be a subtopic of Philosophy (100's). Or to feel the heavy hand of American Protestantism in Religion (200's). Or to wonder why Commerce and Economics are not more closely knit in Sociology (300's). Or to be amazed that Language (400's) is so far from Literature (800's), and Sociology (300's) so far from History (900's). Or to ask if Science (500's) and Technology (600's) are really so clearly distinct. Or to laugh at queer things like Amusements in the Fine Arts (700's). Or to show that Description and Travel are inconveniently placed in History (900's). Et cetera, et cetera, and et cetera.

All these complaints and many more are easy. They are also beside the point, for Melvil Dewey's decimals have worked. Perhaps a "skoolboy" cannot "quikly master it," but master it he does enough to find the books he needs. Today most American libraries use call numbers from the Dewey Decimal Classification, and it is found in some form in almost every country in the world.

In Melvil Dewey we have a hard-boiled realist: "Detaild explanation of selection and arranjement of the many thousand heds wud be tedius; but everywhere filosofic theory and accuracy hav yielded to practical usefulness. The imposibility of making a satisfactory clasifi-cation of all knowlej as preservd in books, has been appreciated from the first, and theoretic harmony and exactness hav been repeatedly sacrificed to practical requirements" (Dewey in DDC 17, p.71).

So "decimals hav been uzed as servants, not as masters . . . The skeme givs us for each topic, as it wer, a case of 9 pijeonholes, with a larj space at the top; and we uze them as every practical business man uzes such pijeonholes about his desk. If, as in 220, there ar les than 9 main topics, it is often convenient to uze the extra spaces for subdivisions" (Dewey in DDC 17, p.76-77).

Finally, consider the parable of the army: "If the soldiers ar ded and in the cemetery they ar as eazily found by fixt as by relativ loca-tion. But if the army is alive and militant, as every library or private working collection o't to be, its resources shud be *findabl* whether in camp, on march or in action" (Dewey in DDC 17, p.78).

Dewey's decimals gave the library relative location; where the decimals left holes the relative index would fill them in. Libraries "alive and militant"; "*findabl*" books; "practical usefulness not filosofic theory and accuracy"—what Cutter called "convenience of the public" tramps roughshod through the decimals.

Interlude: Cutter's Expansive Classification (EC)

"I have been led to prepare a scheme applicable to collections of every size, from the village library in its earliest stages to the national library with a million volumes" (quoted by Sayers, p.142). This was Cutter's ambitious aim, and, although his Expansive Classification (EC) received wide praise, he was to gain his goal only in some small respect and indirectly for the last part: classification for a na-tional library.

EC was a scheme in seven different versions. The first was quite elementary; the seventh (uncompleted at his death in 1903) would have applied to a library of ten million volumes. The term "expansive" did not mean that the notation derived from the first scheme could simply be expanded into the second and then the third, etc., as a library grew larger; instead, "expansive" meant only that EC was de-signed in a series of schedules of increasing fullness. The first scheme, for instance, used only A, B, E, H, L, X, Y, and YF for its main classes; and as the final version neared completion, all letters of the alphabet were used, some of them for subdivisions of classes represented by other letters in earlier versions. The first six classifications were pub-lished in 1893 with a temporary index indicating the place of a particular subject in each of the six schemes. Cutter proposed to publish a full index, possibly with annotations, with his seventh classification.

Cutter considered the order of his classes and subdivisions to be evolutionary; by adopting the alphabet for his main classes and their subdivisions, he was able to achieve a briefer and yet much more specific notation than DDC's decimals would allow. Numerals provided further subdivision by form (1–9) and by place (11–999). Final subdivision was alphabetical by author, using a "Cutter number," which consisted of the initial of the author's surname followed by one or more decimal figures. Cutter's original table provided only two figures, but Kate E. Sanborn later developed the Cutter-Sanborn three-figure table.

"Cutter produced the best classification of the nineteenth century" (LaMontagne, p.215). But he died before he could complete it, and there was no organization (as in the case of DDC) to keep it up to date and to push its use. Only a few libraries use EC today. It is ironic that Cutter's name has survived chiefly in the term "Cutter number" (used generally with DDC) and in the manufactured verb "cuttering," used to designate the process of applying a book number of any kind.

When LC was surveying classification possibilities at the turn of the century, a committee visited libraries using DDC or EC, and they called on Dewey and Cutter to propose certain changes in their systems. Cutter was "perfectly willing to make any changes which after careful consideration seemed necessary," but Dewey "absolutely refused to make any" because of the "inconvenience which would result to the large number of libraries" using DDC. Charles Martel later reported to the Librarian of Congress that DDC had been adopted in only a few large libraries and then often with considerable modification. The chief defects of DDC, Martel said, were: (1) disproportionate allotment of space, (2) unscientific arrangement, (3) arbitrary division and subdivision by tens, and (4) disinclination to change these defects. He concluded: "As the system grows older without change these faults become more serious and aggravating and fewer libraries will be inclined to take them into the bargain. With respect to all of them Cutter's EC is superior, while offering the same advantages as far as may be derived from employing a ready made scheme" (LaMontagne, p.232–33). LC then went ahead to develop its own scheme, but the influence of EC on that scheme was not inconsiderable.

Library of Congress Classification (LCC)

"The system devised has not sought to follow strictly the scientific order of subjects. It has sought rather convenient sequences of the various groups, considering them as groups of books, not as groups of mere subjects."

So wrote Herbert Putnam in his *Annual Report* as Librarian of Congress for 1901. Work on the Library of Congress Classification (LCC) had begun; today the first draft of the entire scheme is not yet complete. In at least three ways America's second popular classification scheme differs from its predecessor begun twenty-five years before:

1. *Purpose.* DDC was intended for use in any library of any size. LCC sought only to arrange the several million books in the nation's largest library. DDC was developed to fit a notation. LCC was developed to fit a particular group (or set of groups) of books, and if the provisional classification with which work in an area began proved faulty, the scheme was changed to meet the conditions set by the books.

2. *History.* DDC was the invention of one man who for many years controlled its development and whose influence still pervades its development. LCC is a confederation of special schemes each developed in detail by a team of subject specialists. DDC could thus be issued in one or two volumes; LCC, however, has been issued in many volumes, each on a single class or part of a class, and published as it was completed. DDC has many mnemonic devices for "divide like" areas, perhaps because one mind devised the scheme as an integrated whole. LCC has few mnemonic devices, because the various major sections developed in detail at different times under different people and in different directions. LCC schedules are, as a result, bulky; DDC is, by comparison, slim. DDC had from the first a relative index of the entire scheme. LCC has only a relative index for each published class (there are no indexes for some parts of P).

3. *Call Numbers.* DDC provided relative location because it was decimally divided throughout; this meant a base of ten major classes. LCC (like EC) used a sort of "decimalism" but applied it to the letters of the alphabet. This meant a possible base of twenty-six main classes. Each main class could be subdivided by use of a second alphabet, e.g., main class A (General Works. Polygraphy.) could have subclasses AA through AZ. Each such subclass (unlike EC) could have its own subclasses numbered arithmetically (*not* decimally) 1 through 9999. Expansion could be in one of three ways: (1) Gaps. Throughout the system gaps were left. Five letters were left vacant in the sequence for main classes, and in each of the first set of subclasses (e.g., AA–AZ) often no more than half of the alphabet was used. In the arithmetical numbering (1–9999) of the divisions of these lettered subclasses, there were more gaps. (Thus even sequential

location offered a sort of relative location.) (2) The Alphabet. Further subdivision of the numbered subclasses might be alphabetical; e.g., in the section for "Chemistry. Metals" we have QD 181 Special topics, A–Z. (3) Decimals. At many points decimals provide further subdivisions; e.g., QL 638 (Zoology. Fishes. Teleostei.) may be further divided to produce QL 638.1 Cyclomstomi; QL 638.2 Dipnoi; and so on. Thus, speaking very broadly, LCC call numbers (like EC call numbers) can provide greater detail and are at the same time often shorter than DDC call numbers.

Purpose, history, call numbers—much of the difference is in detail only. In two important ways DDC and LCC are alike: (1) Both provide relative location. (2) Both are, first of all, practical book shelving devices. DDC and LCC are alike in a third way: They share many of the same problems. We shall examine in detail some of these problems.

Classification of What?

Do we classify knowledge or do we arrange books? It is sometimes said that Dewey began by classifying knowledge and LC began by arranging a particular group of books. In the nineteenth century Edward Edwards tried to distinguish between library classification systems with a metaphysical basis and those which sought only practical, useful arrangements. You will sometimes hear this distinction made today. The problem, that is to say, is philosophy vs. practical needs. Or Bacon vs. Brunet.

We begin with Bacon. In the 1858 classified catalog of the St. Louis Mercantile Library Association, E. W. Johnston announced that "the method . . . is the Baconian . . . It places all books . . . under three great divisions: those of History (or the *Memory*)—of Philosophy (or the *Reason* . . .)—and of Poetry (or the *Imagination*)." He added a class: "Polygraphs, or writers on many things" (LaMontagne, p.162). His three main classes were, indeed, those of Bacon's *Advancement of Learning*.

The "eminent practical success" of Johnston's catalog led W. T. Harris to attempt a classified catalog of the St. Louis Public School Library along the lines of Johnston's general plan. Dewey in turn based his classes on the divisions worked out by Harris.

Now it is possible, as some writers on classification have done, to show Dewey's descent from Bacon in tabular form somewhat as follows (based on LaMontagne, p.182. The main classes in each scheme are in italics and, where appropriate, the numbering of Dewey's main classes follows within parentheses the corresponding classes or subclasses of Johnston and Harris):

BACON (1605)	JOHNSTON (1858)	HARRIS (1870)	DEWEY (1876)
History	History (9)	Science	0 General Works
	Philosophy	Philosophy (1)	1 Philosophy
	Theology (2)	Theology (2)	2 Religion
		Social and	3 Sociology
		Political Sciences (3)	
	Jurisprudence ⎱	Jurisprudence	
	Political Science ⎬ (3)	Politics	
	Political Economy ⎰	Political Economy	
		Education	
		Philology (4)	4 Philology
	Philosophy Proper (1)		
	Natural Sciences (5)	Natural Sciences (5)	5 Natural Sciences
	and	and	
	Useful Arts (6)	Useful Arts (6)	6 Useful Arts
	Education (3)		
	Philology (4)		
Poesy	Poetry	Art	
	Literature (8)	Fine Arts (7)	7 Fine Arts
	Fine Arts (7)	Literature (8)	8 Literature
Philosophy		History (9)	9 History
	Polygraphs (0)	Miscellany (0)	

But the Baconian ancestry of Dewey's ideas is not quite as simple as these neat tables make it. For instance, under History, Bacon included Natural History as well as Civil History, and under Civil History he included Orations, Letters, and Apophthegms. Indeed, each of the four men had somewhat different notions of the content of the classes he listed and of the exact meaning of the terms with which he named those classes. Both Johnston and Harris changed the sequence of Bacon's main classes, and each of the three nineteenth-century classifiers had a different notion about what were main classes and how subclasses should be arranged.

Even if the descent were exact in every detail, would that make Dewey's scheme "philosophical"? Harris used Johnston's scheme not because it was sound philosophy, but because it enjoyed "eminent *practical* success"; and Dewey stated firmly that in his decimals "theoretic harmony and exactness" had time and again yielded to "practical requirements." Finally, in spite of Johnston's appeal to Bacon, the Johnston scheme also looked a lot like that of Brunet (LaMontagne, p.163):

Theology
Jurisprudence
Sciences and Arts
    Philosophy

Economics
Political Science
Natural Sciences
Arts and Crafts
   Writing and Printing
   Fine Arts
   Useful Arts
   Recreative Arts
Language and Literature
History

Jacques-Charles Brunet based this scheme on the System of the Paris Booksellers in the early nineteenth century. It is the custom to say that Brunet and his predecessors were concerned not with philosophy but only with the arrangement of books or the entries for books in a catalog or bibliography. Yet many who have used the Brunet scheme call it also logical; one such philosophical defense moves along these lines (Sayers, p.98–99):

1. *Theology*: Man first of all beholds and deals with God.
2. *Jurisprudence*: He then returns to earth and deals fairly with other men.
3. *Sciences and Arts*: He then turns to himself and the world about him.
4. *Language and Literature*: He seeks to tell what he has learned and to tell it beautifully.
5. *History*: He then seeks to learn what has brought about the world he lives in and what may be that world's destiny.

Classification of knowledge vs. classification of books; philosophy vs. practical needs, Bacon vs. Brunet—have we a real distinction here? It is true that over the years DDC has developed numbers for which few books have appeared and that DDC has failed to develop numbers in areas where many books have been published: this one might expect in a purely philosophical scheme. It is also true that the first edition of a published class in LCC did apply closely to a specific group of books. But the moment *another* book was added to this original LCC collection and classified, or the moment *another* library decided to use the published LCC schedule for its own books, that moment the LCC schedule became "philosophical" and "theoretical" for the one new LC book or for the one non-LC library. For the one new LC book or the one non-LC library collection of books would have to be fitted into the framework of an already determined schedule. As time passed and more and more new books came to either library, gaps and underdeveloped areas and overdeveloped areas would turn up in LCC just as they have turned up in DDC.

Do we classify knowledge or do we arrange books? In the everyday work of an American library it is a distinction without a difference.

Notation

Notation is the set of symbols by means of which we translate a classification scheme into call numbers. It is the custom to say something like this: "Notation is a thing apart. *First* of all, draw up a classification scheme; then devise a Notation to express it." But suppose we did not have Dewey's story of the "long sermon by Pres. Stearns" and the birth of the great idea. It would still be hard to believe that one day Dewey sat down at a desk and drew up a list of the main classes of knowledge with their divisions and subdivisions—and *then* jumped to his feet and shouted: "By golly! They are all in tens! I can mark them with decimals!" The hard fact is that call numbers are the written language of a classification scheme. In this language we tell how to arrange books on shelves according to the classes and subclasses of the classification scheme.

This call number language is like any other language in at least two ways:

1. It limits what we can write. You may have in your head the most wonderful poem since Homer, but if you cannot find the language for it, it stays in your head.

2. It can be understood easily only if its symbols are understood easily. The symbols are, of course, notation. The classification scheme is something which the library user does not understand; he may not even know it exists. If the notation symbols are to translate the classification scheme into call numbers the user *can* understand, the notation must have a meaning and a sequence quite apart from the meaning and sequence of the classification scheme and—even more important —quite easily understood by the user. Else he will never find a book by himself.

These two restrictions seem to limit notation to arabic numerals or the letters of the alphabet. If we adopt arabic numerals as the symbols of our notation, the numerals will arrange the classes of our classification scheme. We can, of course, choose *which* class gets what number; but if, like Dewey, we adopt decimals for subclasses, we are limited to ten subclasses for each class and ten sub-subclasses for each subclass. (We can have more than ten main classes if we wish.) Or, if we adopt the roman alphabet, the letters will arrange the classes, and we are limited to twenty-six main classes. Here also we can decide *which* class gets which letter, but if we use letters for the subclasses, we are again limited to twenty-six subclasses for each main class.

Whether we choose arabic numerals or roman alphabet, we are, to use Dewey's comparison (see above p.100), equipping each topic of our classification scheme with a fixed number of pigeonholes. The number of these pigeonholes may be exactly that of the parts of the topic; more than likely we shall come out, as Dewey suggests, with too many or too few pigeonholes. And then, "If, as in 220, ther ar les than 9 main topics, it is often convenient to uze the extra spaces for subdivisions." Now in such a case it is possible to print the classification scheme in such a way as to show by *indention* (or some other device) which are the topics and which are the subtopics. But the user of the library will not see these indentions (often, alas, the classifier may miss them), nor will the user of the library care *so long as the call numbers lead to the books.* Thus, for all practical purposes, the notation or call numbers are not merely a translation of the classification scheme. To the user the notation or call numbers *are* the classification scheme.

We shall look briefly at some other notions about notation. If a notation consistently employs only one kind of symbol (as in DDC), it is said to be a *pure* notation. If it employs (as in LCC) more than one kind of symbol, it is a *mixed* notation. Some people believe that pure notation is better, but pure notation limits the number of subclasses at each level. DDC, for instance, is limited to ten; LCC with its mixed notation may have 9999 subclasses of each of its two-letter divisions.

Brevity is helpful in call numbers. In general, if the notation provides a large number of main classes (as in LCC), brevity is much more apt to result because there is no need to subdivide in such great detail, as in DDC where there are only ten main classes.

Notation is said to be good if it is flexible, that is, if it can easily provide call numbers for new subjects admitted to the classification scheme. DDC is not flexible in its main classes and their subclasses; new subjects can be admitted only by further decimal division of already existing numbers, and this results in rather long call numbers. LCC is flexible only because some letters and some numbers have been left vacant at various levels. Even this is not complete flexibility: LCC could, for instance, admit a whole new main class at X; but perhaps this main class would come logically between P and Q.

Some people think that mnemonic features are good in notation. DDC is mnemonic rather frequently, e.g., the form divisions (standard subdivisions beginning with DDC 17), the linguistic numbers, and the geographical numbers. LCC has rather few mnemonic devices. It has not been scientifically proved how useful such features are.

Bias

Both LCC and DDC have bias in many respects. DDC, for instance, is Protestant (cf. the 200's) and Anglo-Saxon (cf. the 900's).

LCC serves the needs of the United States first (cf. D with E–F). To some extent bias in a classification scheme is the necessary result of its history; for instance, LCC seeks to serve only LC, and its outlook naturally reflects the bias of a collection built to serve Congress primarily. To a lesser extent the same sort of defense applies to DDC; it was designed to serve American libraries and even yet American libraries are its chief users. Consequently, DDC will be most useful if it reflects the bias of the collections in American libraries.

Obviously we can overcome bias in a classification scheme by changing the scheme. In a non-Anglo-Saxon, non-Protestant country such as India, DDC might be more useful if the numbers for the United States were used for India and the numbers for Christianity were used for Indian religions. The same principle might apply in adapting LCC.

Bias raises a basic question about classification schemes: Can we have a universally useful universal classification scheme? Or will the bias of the scheme's builder always limit the ability of the scheme to serve *all* subjects and *all* peoples?

Change

We have seen that change is a major problem in other areas of cataloging. Change of an author's name, change of a serial's title, change of the title of any work in its various editions, change in the name of a subject or in the relation of that subject to other subjects— we have to deal with change every day. Change is also a major problem with call numbers.

DDC was the product of the late nineteenth century; LCC, of the early twentieth century. Since DDC and LCC were first drawn up, the revolution in knowledge has been tremendous. How can the schemes be changed to accommodate it? The debate is usually described in terms of two slogans: (1) "Integrity of numbers" and (2) "Keeping pace with knowledge." Both schemes have the problem, but it is more noticeable in DDC for at least two reasons: (1) DDC is the older; therefore, it has had more time to get out of date. (2) More librarians complain about DDC simply because more libraries use DDC.

Almost from the beginning "integrity of numbers" was a basic policy of DDC. DDC 2 (1885) was much enlarged and it had changed some eighty or ninety class numbers from DDC 1. Dewey assured librarians that this edition "may be considered as having the numbers settled" (Mills, p.57). (Like the promise of Noah after the Flood.) In the years which followed, Dewey was as good as his word. When LC was casting about for a new classification, DDC was considered; but Dewey refused to make the rather considerable changes in his scheme which the Library felt would be necessary (see p.101). The proposed changes, he argued, would be too inconvenient for the many libraries already using DDC. He repeated his original promise several times: e.g., in 1926 "A shifting classification is impracticable for libraries," and at the end of his life, "Our rule for 50 years is best, stick by old numbers and provide for new subjects by attaching them to the most nearly allied." (*Journal of Cataloging and Classification*, 12:200 [Oct. 1956]).

So, through the fourteenth edition, DDC grew steadily in bulk; and call numbers based on DDC grew in length. Yet neither grew greatly in quality.

DDC 15 (1951, called the "Standard Edition") was a revolution. A great deal of money (more than $100,000) had gone into it. There had been a questionnaire which showed that many libraries (even large libraries) wanted simplification. It was the golden age of simplification: The greatly simplified LC rules for description had just appeared (1949), and work was going ahead on simplifying rules for entry. Library associations, outside experts, and individual librarians all agreed: simplification. So simplification there was: New expansions where they would "keep pace with knowledge." Ruthless cutting away of "superfluities" (4621 numbers as compared with 31,444 in Edition 14). Relocations (1015 of them from provisions of Edition 14). Notation cut back to five or six digits. Index greatly shortened. Modern, everyday English instead of Dewey's "simplified" spelling (always forbidding to the novice) and sometimes antiquated terms.

The counterrevolution was swift and loud and bloody. The schedules were too brief and sometimes obscure; the Index was too brief and sometimes misleading. But worst of all, "integrity of numbers" was no more and this would mean reclassification. The large research libraries growled that this would eat time and money. Therefore DDC 15 revised (1953) had fuller tables and doubled the Index.

DDC 16 (1958) looked more like DDC 14: the digits were back in strength and the Index was full. In fact, the Index filled a separate volume. But DDC was still in everyday English; much more important, the *detail* of the digits was much more evenly developed. DDC 15 had contained 1015 relocations from provisions of DDC 14; DDC 16 had 985 from DDC 14 and 618 from DDC 15, for a total of 1603. After a bow to the past, DDC 16 had consolidated many gains of the revolution in DDC 15.

DDC 17 continued to look to the present and the future. There were 746 relocations from provisions of DDC 16; there was even some relocation in area concepts, a rather drastic change because every heading in DDC can be subdivided geographically. DDC 17 had "new or renewed emphasis on subject integrity and subject relationships"

(Introd. 5.1). The scheme drew a sharp line between "discipline" and "subject": "There is no one place for any subject in itself; a subject may appear in any or all of the disciplines." "No class can be said to cover the scope of marriage, or water, or tomatoes, or Brazil . . ." Thus a work on marriage belongs in 301 if it handles sociological aspects: 155, psychological; 173, ethical; 234 or 265, sacramental (Christian); 296, Jewish; 297, Islamic; 390, marriage customs; 613, hygiene; 700 or 800, subject of art or literature, and so on. (Introd. 2.21). Among other striking features of this edition were a long-overdue, completely new schedule for "Psychology" (150); the table of "standard subdivisions" (more appropriately named than the old "form divisions"); and a separate "area table." For the first time, DDC 17 made a determined effort to ease the problems created by DDC's Protestant, Anglo-Saxon, U.S.A. bias. Finally, there was the notable conclusion of the editors and the Decimal Classification Editorial Policy Committee: "A reasonable amount of continuing change through relocation is not only desirable but inevitable" (Introd. 5.132). There were, of course, also flaws: The Introduction, for example, was quite long and involved and it had no index; and the Index to the schedules was often more pedagogical than helpful. Such defects can, of course, be corrected in later editions; indeed, revision began at once with the publication of a new index for DDC 17.

In editing DDC at least three forces are at work:

1. *The Editor.* Benjamin A. Custer was editor of DDC 16 and DDC 17.

2. *The Library of Congress.* In 1924, Dewey turned over the copyrights of DDC to a charitable trust he set up, the Lake Placid Club Education Foundation, with Forest Press, a subsidiary of the Foundation, serving as publisher. In 1927, LC gave space to the DDC editorial office, and beginning in 1930, DDC numbers appeared on certain LC printed cards. In January 1954, at the request of the ALA Division of Cataloging and Classification and with the concurrence of the Forest Press, LC took over administration of the DDC editorial office. Since then DDC 16 and DDC 17 have appeared.

3. *The Decimal Classification Editorial Policy Committee* (DCEPC). Since the 1930's there has been some sort of liaison between ALA and the DDC editorial office. DCEPC is a joint committee of the ALA and the Foundation, composed almost entirely of librarians and providing representation for the Library of Congress and Forest Press.

DDC 17 provoked a violent reaction. A storm of articles asked "Is Dewey Dead?" (cf. *Library Journal,* 91:4035–37 [Sept. 15, 1966]), and many libraries began to think of joining the "flight from Dewey" to LCC. DDC has always aroused great emotion; DDC 17 was no exception. In such an atmosphere it was helpful to have Phyllis Rich-

mond's sensible note in the *Library Journal* (91:4870 [Oct. 15, 1966])
pointing out that libraries cannot use either LCC or DDC call numbers uncritically just as they appear on LC cards. Later a sober, objective article by William J. Welsh (*Library Resources and Technical
Services,* 11:345–53 [1967]) showed in detail that LCC "schedules
are being revised constantly, literally every day," and he cited the
extent of this revision by statistics of class numbers established and
changed in recent fiscal years:

YEAR	ESTABLISHED	CHANGED
1963–64	1,803	259
1964–65	2,218	442
1965–66	2,233	218

Moreover, these changes are not immediately applied retroactively
to titles cataloged prior to the changes; and for some time it had
been necessary to keep most schedules in print by simply issuing
reprints with supplementary pages containing the additions and
changes.

LCC is, indeed, somewhat freer to "keep pace with knowledge."
It is responsible to only one library; theoretically, any change is
possible, provided LC is willing. But if more and more libraries
come to use LCC, pressure may build here also for "integrity of numbers." "Keeping pace with knowledge" is said to cost money; "integrity
of numbers" is said to save money. Both statements are true, particularly if the call numbers already on books are changed to meet new
schedules. But so does a haircut or a new car cost money. Yet few
people try to save money by avoiding the haircut or the new car if
the style they have is badly out of date.

Moreover, with regard to some aspects of library service, the dispute
is largely academic. Call numbers are, after all, primarily finding
devices; and books can be found even if their call numbers are an-
tique. Perhaps it is necessary to "keep pace with knowledge" only
in those areas of the stacks where browsing is a major consideration.
Perhaps older books can then be retired (*without* changed call numbers) to closed stacks.

"Integrity of numbers" vs. "keeping pace with knowledge"—the debate raises a basic question: What is the function of a new edition
of a classification scheme? Imperative or suggestive? Imperative is
just that: Change all the call numbers in the library at once. Suggestive is milder: If any part of the edition now in use is giving trouble,
it may help to see this new edition's suggestion in that area. Probably,
even in the good old days before DDC 15, many large libraries considered new editions only suggestive.

Reclassification

The new edition of a classification scheme is only one temptation the cataloger faces on the high mountain of classification. The other two are more dangerous:

1. For a small library growing rapidly larger should we move from the cramping decimals of DDC to the broad vistas of LCC? Probably not, particularly if the already classified collection is large. Both schemes, as we have seen, have their advantages; neither scheme is perfect. There is little concrete evidence that one scheme really serves the user of such a library better than the other, or at least that it serves enough better to pay for the change. For the cost of reclassification can be tremendous, both in thousands of dollars and in years and even decades of time.

2. If a library has a nineteenth-century scheme (or a homemade scheme) that has not been kept up to date by regular new editions, should it change to DDC or LCC? Probably yes, if for no other reason than because of the great saving in being able to use the call numbers printed on LC and Wilson cards and in the *Publishers' Weekly–American Book Publishing Record* entries.

What about wholesale reclassification? Consider Ranganathan's approach: "osmosis." Studies of use suggest that the most-used books are recent books. For example, beginning today the cataloger might classify every new book by DDC or LCC. As books on loan (i.e., the actively used books) are returned, they are reclassified. Other books which enjoy active use may be reclassified. After the first months of high pressure, the daily stream of books to be reclassified will begin to recede. Eventually the library will have a stable collection of old books still arranged by the old scheme, but they will cause little trouble because they will be little used. The active collection will have up-to-date call numbers which cost less than the do-it-yourself variety.

It may be that complete osmosis will not fit a particular library's problem; but even a modified osmosis will be easier than a complete reclassification on the budget and on the bodies and souls of the classifiers. For complete reclassification means: (1) remove, revise, and then refile all cards; (2) find all books, check them against the cards, reclassify them, relabel them, and then reshelve them; (3) maintain usual service to readers; and (4) keep current with cataloging new books. Without a lot of time and money, and brawn, brains, and patience the cataloger cannot do it. Is it worth the cost?

The Second Objective Again

Relative location, we have said, answers the second objective, to help the user find all books of a kind together. At the same time, relative location means shifting location. Every time a truckload of newly cataloged books goes to the stacks, someone may have to move a shelf, or even a section of shelves of books, to make room for some of them. It takes staff time to keep the books moving in this way. Also it means that in planning stack area much more shelving space must be allowed than will actually be needed so that intershelving will be as easy a job as possible.

Then there is the user. Relative location and the second objective really help the user only if the stacks are open so that he can browse, and only to the extent that books he wants or may want are on the shelves. If many of the really desirable books on a subject are in use (at a cubicle or signed out) and if many of those which remain are out of date or in a foreign language, the user may gain little from this costly second objective.

Even if the books are all there, the user's problems are not over. If the call numbers are based on a subject classification such as DDC and LCC, each call number stands for a specific subject. This raises the same two problems we found with the specific subject heading (p.79–80 above):

1. The specific subject of a book is a unity in itself, but
2. The specific subject of that book is also part of a broader subject which may itself be the specific subject of another book.

All of which means that if call numbers were completely to answer the second objective (to help the user find all books of a kind together), they should in some way call attention not only to all books on the particular subject in which the user is interested, but also to books on broader subjects which contain substantial material on the narrower subject. This reference would be a sort of third objective for call numbers such as the third objective for subject headings.

With the direct and specific subject heading we found that the only way yet devised to meet the third objective was Cutter's syndetic apparatus. We further found that in practice this syndetic feature is costly, awkward, and, indeed, seldom even attempted consistently. The third objective, then, is difficult with subject headings; with call numbers it seems to be impossible.

This problem also is often phrased in a slogan: "Close classification vs. broad classification." Close classification means to apply to a book the call number which stands for that book's specific subject. Broad classification means to use call numbers which stand for only broader subjects; this means that in some cases the call number on a book stands for a subject which includes that book's subject along with other subjects.

Both DDC and LCC provide for close classification, although LCC's larger number of main classes means that, like EC, it can achieve close classification with somewhat shorter call numbers. DDC 15 provided only broad classification when it limited the number of digits to five or six. DDC 16, however, returned to close classification with adoption of the principle that "the existence in American libraries of more than twenty titles which would fall in a given number raises a presumption in favor of subdivision." Speaking broadly, DDC is more flexible than LCC in this matter. LCC must supply close classification; with DDC there is a choice, and now that LC cards provide segmented DDC numbers that choice is relatively easy.

Many smaller libraries seem to provide good service using only the abridged editions of DDC and the Sears lists of subject headings; both provide only for broad subjects. Are close classification and specific subject headings really useful?

In 1937 there appeared a remarkable book, Grace Kelley's *The Classification of Books: An Enquiry into Its Usefulness to the Reader.* Taking three subjects (Beaver, Buffalo, Cormorant) as examples, she found that, of all the material in the University of Chicago library on these subjects, there was on the library shelves under the specific call number for each only 5.9, 2.2, and 5.7 percent respectively. Of entries under specific subject headings for these subjects in the catalog, only about one third were for books shelved under the subject's class number.

Perhaps close classification is not as useful as we have assumed, even in large research libraries. Suppose, for instance, that subject A may be subdivided into subjects B, C, and D, and we use close classification. There have been written, to use DDC's idea of twenty books, fifteen to twenty books on each of B, C, and D. The call number for D will locate all the books on that topic alone, but there may be some excellent material on D included in books on subject A as a whole. Between the D books and the A books there may be as many as forty books on B and C. Of course, there will be books on the relation of subject D to subject K or subject X or both; they may be shelved a long way off indeed. And if, instead of three subdivisions of A, we have many, the problem gets worse. Nor can we fall back on the catalog and specific subject headings. Even if the catalog keeps up a consistent syndetic system, there will be "see also" references from A to B, C, and D each, but none from B, C, and D to A.

Suppose we try broad classification. We shall now have eighty books—some on A, some on B, some on C, some on D—all intershelved with the one call number for subject A. This means that the one call number will give us more material on D, because it will give us all the books on A which contain material on D as well as all the books on D alone. But this same call number for A also foists on us all the books on B only and all the books on C only.

We return to cost: Close classification probably costs more than broad classification because it demands more time and skill of the classifier to draw these fine lines of separation. It may also cost more time and skill of the shelver because he has more places into which he must fit books.

Close classification vs. broad classification—one cannot have both. Each library tries to find that balance which will best serve its users. No library can prove that it has the perfect answer. No user can depend only on the catalog or the arrangement of the books on the shelves; he must also use bibliographies, other reference works—and his imagination—if he is to hope to find even a good share of the library's material on his subject.

So relative location and the second objective are costly and imperfect devices if call numbers reflect a subject classification. For that reason, fixed location—or at least sequential location—is again coming into use. Shelving in closed stacks by size and/or accession may be enough for little-used books. The catalog can always give some sort of subject approach.

Serials

Both DDC and LCC have slots for serials among various subject classes, and many libraries do use call numbers to shelve their serials by subject. At least three kinds of serials may require some comment: (1) Periodicals, (2) Government Documents, and (3) Monograph Series.

1. *Periodicals.* If the library is relatively small (e.g., a school library or a smaller public library) or if the library's subject is rather limited (e.g., a special library), a simple alphabetical arrangement by title may be better than classification by subject.

Most of the periodicals will be indexed. If the user approaches the periodical collection by means of an index, it is easy for him to find the periodicals to which the index refers him if all periodicals are on the shelf in one alphabet. On the other hand, if periodicals are divided by subject, the user has the intermediate step of looking up call numbers before he can locate the periodicals.

Changed titles complicate subject arrangement. If periodicals have call numbers, these call numbers are probably to be found on a card with entry under the latest title the periodical has. Yet the reference to that periodical in an index will be to the title it held at the time a particular article was indexed. The user will look first in the catalog under that title; if it has changed he finds a cross reference to another title, and loses more time on this intermediate step. If periodicals are shelved by title, each new title will mean a new place on the shelf for those issues of the periodical holding that title.

If the library is large enough to have developed departments, then roughly the same conditions as those in a special library would seem to indicate alphabetical shelving for the periodicals in each department. If periodicals do receive call numbers, probably broad classification is the most useful for the obvious reason that few periodicals deal with a narrow subject; and those which do may change their emphasis with any issue. In large libraries without departments, classification would, of course, bring periodicals in a subject field together with other material in that field.

2. *Government Documents.* Many depository libraries arrange their federal documents by the Superintendent of Documents classification, and a number of schemes have been devised for arranging state and local documents. On the other hand, some libraries, such as LC and the New York Public Library, handle government documents as they would other serials. Broadly speaking, LCC is rather better equipped to deal with documents than is DDC.

To treat documents in a special way is, of course, to segregate them; this means to violate the second objective, to help the user find all books of a kind together. Many valuable books are documents issued by some government; if they do not appear on the shelves with other books, the user will suffer.

3. *Monograph Series.* It is conventional to give one call number to a monograph series. Certainly this is the cheapest way to classify it, and it satisfies the notion that the call number is simply a book-finding device.

Yet obviously this violates the second objective, to help the user find all books of a kind together. Of course, in some few monograph series every monograph would *as a monograph* receive the same call number as the series. Yet if this is the case and if the number of monographs in the series is large, then we ignore the DDC principle of subdivision at the twenty-title point. Thus, whatever may be our practice with close classification in the rest of the stacks, with this group of books we practice broad classification.

The series itself may trip up both cataloger and user. Its monographs may not be numbered; the cataloger must then invent an arbitrary numbering system. Or the monograph may be peculiarly numbered: e.g., the first three volumes of Monograph A may be issued as Volumes 20, 25, and 70 of the monograph series. The user can find all of Monograph A only if he thinks to copy down all three series volume numbers while he is at the catalog.

It all depends on whether we want broad or close classification and whether we want to serve the second objective.

How To Find the Call Number

Call numbers, we have said (see p.106 above), are the language of the classification scheme. DDC and LCC are classification schemes arranged by subject; so first of all, we must know what the book is about.

Writers on classification may say at this point: Wade into the classification scheme. Find the broad topic which includes the subject. Then look for that topic's appropriate subdivision and then look for the subdivision's appropriate subtopic and so on until we have a call number.

This is the front door approach. It is good intellectual exercise, but it is not as easy as it sounds and it may take a great deal of time. There are side doors. DDC has a relative index to the entire classification. This will give the numbers not only for a topic but also for the relation of that topic to other topics, something one might not find with ease wandering through the classification scheme from broader subjects to narrower subjects. LCC has individual indexes for most published schedules.

The subject heading list is another side door. The LC list has LCC numbers after many of its entries, and the Sears list prior to the current edition had DDC numbers after its entries. Printed cards and bibliographies open another side door. LC cards give LCC numbers and often DDC numbers, and Wilson cards give DDC numbers. *American Book Publishing Record* entries also give numbers.

Of course, a side door is only that: a side door. Like the front door, it has done no more than let one into the classification. Like the front door, it has its limitations. The index to a general classification scheme, for instance, tries to index infinity; it cannot hope to name all possible relationships of all possible topics. The same is true of a general subject heading list. No matter how a cataloger has found his number, he will still want to be sure that it stands for an appropriate subtopic of an appropriate topic so that the book will be shelved among other books in whose company the user will be glad to find it.

How does one know that his number is *the* number? There is no shortage of people eager to let us in on the secret. Everyone who writes about classification is eager to tell how to do it. And, of course, there are always Merrill, Sayers (p.234–35), and Sayers-Maltby (p.250–51). Sayers summarized the advice of other people in twelve rules consisting of two series with rules numbered 1–7 and 1–5 respectively; Sayers-Maltby had 1–4 in the second series. (Actually, Sayers considered only his first series to be rules; the second were statements "hardly rules, but which deserve attention.") These rules are below. The numbering is my own with indication of Sayers and Sayers-Maltby numbers; statements in the second series are so indicated: e.g., "Sayers 2d 1" would refer to the first statement in Sayers' second series. After each rule is some comment.

1. *Place a book where it will be most useful.* (Sayers 1)

Merrill 2 is essentially the same except that he calls for a location "permanently useful"; Sayers-Maltby 1 has it "most permanently useful." Merrill 6 tells us to "modify a rule of classification of books when necessary or desirable to meet special needs or types of service." Writers on classification often refer to a particular practice as "helpful" or "unhelpful." Basically, all of this sort of thing is simply another form of Cutter's insistence on the "convenience of the public." Now "useful" or "helpful" (like "home" and "motherhood") is an idea we can all applaud. But useful or helpful to whom? Sayers suggests the "professional workers in the subject we are classing." But how do we find out what they want—and will they agree among themselves?

> 2. *Class by subject, then by form, except in pure literature, where form is paramount.* (Sayers 2)

Sayers-Maltby 2 modifies the exception phrase: "except in the form classes, where the precedence is always given to form." Merrill 3 is more cautious: "Class a book ordinarily by subject." Then he notes that certain other characteristics such as date, binding, language, literary form, and class of reader may on occasion determine the number. All of these and similar topics may also be subdivisions of the subject; Merrill 5b further adds: "Subordinate place to topic."

> 3. *Consider the predominant tendency or purpose of a book.* (Sayers 2d 1; Sayers-Maltby 2d 1)

Merrill 4: "Class a book primarily according to the intent of the author in writing it." But authors, like other people, may not always do precisely what they intend to do: the subject of a book may be different from what the author intended it to be. "Predominant tendency" is probably a sounder approach.

> 4. *Place a book at the most specific head that will contain it.* (Sayers 3; Sayers-Maltby 4)

Merrill 5 also endorses close classification. Difficulties with close classification are considered above (p.114–15).

> 5. *When a book appears on a subject which has no stated place in the classification scheme, determine the heading to which it is most nearly related, and make a place for it there.* (Sayers 6)

Sayers-Maltby 5 is the same, but adds that "the exact application of this rule may depend on whether a new edition of the scheme in question will soon be available or not." But if the book is to be used, it must go somewhere *now*; a nest of unclassified books waiting on a "new edition of the scheme" helps no one. Moreover, the "new edition" will not simply fill gaps in the current edition; if it "keeps pace with knowledge," it may change the meaning of some symbols used in the current edition. The better the classification, the less often gaps should occur. The insertion should, of course, always be in harmony with the spirit of the scheme.

6. *When a book deals with two subjects, classify under the dominant subject; if this cannot be ascertained, class under the first. Likewise, if a book deals with not more than three divisions of the same subject, place it in the one that is most prominently dealt with, or—if the treatment is of equal importance—in the one dealt with first. If the book deals with more divisions of the subject than three, place it at the general heading which covers them all.* (Sayers-Maltby 3)

Sayers 4 consists of only the second sentence of this rule. As to the first sentence, Sayers 2d 2 reads: "Where one subject affects another, or an author influences another, place under the subject or author influenced." Sayers-Maltby omits this rule (Sayers 2d 2) entirely, apparently because the first sentence of Sayers-Maltby 3, with its emphasis on "dominant subject," involves a general problem of which "influence" is only a part. This general problem is what Sayers-Maltby, following Ranganathan, calls "phase analysis": the attempt to list all possible "phase relations" of subjects in two-subject books, and with each such book to determine precisely and readily which of the two subjects is "dominant." We shall look briefly at a few of these phase relations:

Influence Phase. This, of course, is Sayers 2d 2 stated above with decision to "place under the subject or author influence." Merrill 15a and b agree. Yet the rule is rather arbitrary; note Merrill's example: "Economic conditions as a cause of war. Class under war, but class economic *effects* of war under economics." This is drastically to separate discussions of economic conditions. With regard to authors, Merrill 292b agrees with Sayers, but Merrill 292a provides that the "influence of a writer upon a literature" is to be classed with "literary criticism of the author concerned." In a note Merrill tries to justify this inconsistency by "the greater importance of persons. What concerns them individually should be kept together; the individual outweighs the thing"; Mills (p.161) is probably correct in calling this "no particular reason."

Bias Phase. This is to be found in a book on a particular subject written with a "bias" toward the needs of a particular kind of reader. Examples are "Ethics for the Businessman" (Sayers-Maltby, p.254), or "Heraldry for Craftsmen and Designers" (Merrill, 37), or "Psychology for Nurses" (Mills, p.161). Merrill says of his example: "Written to explain to makers of crests and coats of arms the meaning of heraldic language and symbols and *thus a work on heraldry*" (italics are mine). Similarly, Mills suggests that such a book is a *"general introduction* to the subject biased" (Psychology in his example) and should be placed under that subject "where *everybody* interested in the subject will find it"; "under the subject to which it is biased" (Nurses), it will be found by "only a few of the potential users." *Colon Classification* (Part 1, p.56) and Sayers-Maltby agree with such a decision, although Sayers-Maltby expresses misgivings. It does, indeed, seem possible that such a book is *not* a "general introduction" to the subject biased and that it would not, therefore, be wanted by the general user.

Tool Phase. This is illustrated in Merrill 10: "Results attained in a certain field of research: Class under the topic investigated without reference to the character of the data or means employed." It may be that examples of this phase "usually reveal the appropriate placing to us readily enough" (Sayers-Maltby, p.253); and in the example "English History in English Fiction" (Mills, p.161) perhaps, as Mills remarks, English history is "the subject of enquiry" and "it is being studied via the medium of English Fiction." But what of the user who is a student of English fiction?

Comparison Phase and Difference Phase. These occur "when a comparison is made between two subjects" and "when the difference between two subjects is expounded" (*Colon Classification*, Part 1, p.56). Why there should be two kinds of relation here is not clear; in any event, the "First Phase" for each is "the one whose class number is the earlier ordinal number"; that is, selection is arbitrary.

So much for Rule 6. We have here the same major problem we have met elsewhere in cataloging: more than one. The phrases "dominant subject" and "most prominently dealt with" are reminiscent of "principal author" or "author chiefly responsible" (see above p.34) and the "compound" subject heading with its question about which element is named first (see above p.70). We have here also the arbitrary answer when logic fails: falling back to the "one dealt with first" or "the one whose class number is the earlier ordinal number," just as we fall back to the "first named author." Finally, there is the preoccupation with the magic number three. With more than one author or with more than one possible subject heading, we can always rely on added entries. A book can have only one call number. This, of course, makes the selection of a call number terribly important—or, looked at from another point of view, it simply strengthens the argument against close classification.

Rule 6 shows the futility of Rule 1: which subject will be the source of the "most useful" call number? The student of economics —one of Sayers' "professional workers in the subject"—may not want books on economic conditions as causes of this-and-that so far from books on economic conditions as results of this-and-that. The student of Milton may want books on Milton's influence on John Doe alongside other books on Milton. Phase analysis is little help. Any solution may be arbitrary, and Rule 6 thus often becomes an illustration of Rule 7 which follows.

> 7. *When two headings clash, make a decision as to which is to prevail.* (Sayers 5)

Sayers-Maltby 7 is the same and adds: "Record this decision for future reference." The meaning of "clash" is not entirely clear; one would expect the two subjects to have some relation to each other. If there is a relation, Rule 6 or 8—or something of the sort—should help determine the call number. Even so, the arbitrary imperative, "make a decision," is quite practical. If the cataloger cannot decide between two numbers, it is possible that the user would have as much trouble deciding. Better to stick *some* sort of number on the book and get it into the catalog and onto the shelf than to spend long hours weighing philosophical niceties.

> 8. *Books pro and con any subject go together at the subject.* (Sayers 2d 3; Sayers-Maltby 2d 2)

Merrill 7 supplements this rule: "Facts or data of whatever kind" used to prove a point or policy are to be ignored. What counts is the topic to be proved. Merrill 9 would class a work "contrasting two opinions" under the opinion advocated by the author. But Merrill 80a would class under the topic "without reference to the author's point of view" a book on a theological doctrine, e.g., a book on the Trinity written by a Unitarian. Yet attitude toward the Trinity is one of the things which determine the Unitarian position. Sayers' simple statement in our Rule 8 of what seems obvious is thus not so simple in practice. At times it is in a way simply the "tool phase" (see above, Rule 6); at times it may become quite arbitrary.

> 9. *Avoid placings which are in the nature of criticism.* (Sayers 7; Sayers-Maltby 6)

This, of course, merely restates a general rule for all the cataloger's work: Do not pass judgment on books; describe them.

> 10. *Always have a reason for your placing of a book.* (Sayers 2d 4; Sayers-Maltby 2d 3)

Who will admit he has no reason for what he is doing, and who, when pressed, will be unable to find *some* reason?

> 11. *Index all decisions.* (Sayers 2d 5)

Sayers-Maltby 2d 4 adds that "this will make the practice of your library clear to its future classifiers and will enable a system to be applied in a consistent manner." Consistency is indeed important, especially when logic has failed.

So much for Sayers, Sayers-Maltby, and Merrill; their rules are rather general. There are also at least two specific rules to be added:

12. *Check the introduction to the classification scheme.*

In addition to the Introduction to DDC 16, there is the *Guide to the Use of the Dewey Decimal Classification* (1962) based on practice in assigning DDC numbers to LC cards; what is pertinent in this *Guide* was incorporated in DDC 17. For LCC the final chapters of La-Montagne may be helpful.

13. *Check the call number in the shelf list.*

Has this call number been used for books of this kind in the past? Even though it may not be exactly the "correct" call number, it can at least be consistent.

These are some answers to the question: How does one know that his call number is *the* number? As with subject headings, it is fairly easy to deal with a book with only one, clearly stated subject. Problems come with the book with more than one subject, each with more or less relation to the other. Again, as with subject headings, the answer to the problem is usually arbitrary rather than logical. For the answer generally simply states practice. Sayers seeks a consensus of writers on classification; Merrill relies heavily on what classifiers say they have done. In addition, there is the customary bow to the user (Rule 1), the platitude (Rule 10), and the practical requirement that the cataloger at least be consistent in his inconsistencies (Rules 7, 11, 12, and 13).

Book Numbers

Thus far we have dealt with the call number as though it consisted only of a set of symbols derived from a classification scheme and indicating the subject of the book. Usually the call number includes also a book number. The book number shows just where its book is to be shelved among the other books with the same classification subject number. Generally the arrangement is alphabetical by the family names of the authors, but it may also be alphabetical by subject (as with the subject of a biography) or chronological by date of writing or publication. Beneath the book number there may be another number providing further subarrangement by title (if the author has written more than one book on the subject), or by date (if there has been more than one edition), or by author (if the first element of the book number was for subject). Further refinements are possible to indicate translations, criticisms, biography, bibliography, etc.

There is a wide variety of practice in constructing book numbers. A few of the major ideas are listed below.

The Cutter number or the Cutter-Sanborn number is derived from a table (see p.101 above).

The LC scheme, devised to go with LCC subject numbers, is more flexible and generally shorter than the Cutter scheme. It begins with a simple base of an initial letter followed by one figure; this figure may be expanded decimally. The LC book number is generally shorter than Cutter or Cutter-Sanborn because, as a rule, the LCC subject numbers provide close classification. This means that under each there may be only a few authors. (LC book numbers are not to be confused with LCC alphabetical subdivision of numbered subclasses; see p.103 above.)

Book numbers derived from the Biscoe table will produce a chronological arrangement; this is helpful with any subject—e.g., science or technology—in which date may often be as important as author. A Biscoe number could, of course, be added beneath a number for the author or subject, or the actual date may be used.

There are various other schemes. For a relatively small collection one may use only the initial, or perhaps the first two or three letters, of the author's last name. Or the name may be spelled out completely. Or there may be no book number at all. In that case, the information printed on the spine of the book provides the subarrangement, and it leads to a certain amount of confusion. Anything less than a Cutter, Cutter-Sanborn, or LC book number may result in the library's having more than one book with the same call number. This may not hinder the user, although it may make the library's records somewhat confused.

Panacea

Most American libraries arrange their books with call numbers derived from DDC or LCC. These are subject classifications, and they have certain major problems not unlike the problems with subject headings. Close classification, for instance, like a direct and specific subject heading, fails to reveal much that the library has on a specific subject. Classification of a book with more than one subject is as involved as the compound subject heading. A classification scheme, like a list of subject headings, must adapt to change in the name and content of subjects and in their relation to other subjects. Just as with subject headings, the answers to these problems tend to be pragmatic and ad hoc rather than logical and consistent. To some extent, DDC and LCC, like subject headings lists, just grow.

Now all this is not so bad as long as we think (as has been our custom in American libraries) that the call number is simply a device by which we know where to shelve a book and where to go to get it later. As long as our books are in *some* order, why waste time and money on *what* order?

But some of us want more from classification. Surely it can do more than just find books somewhere or other? Surely we can think up an answer to its problems? Surely we shall be helping the user if we do? About this point the questions become affirmative statements in a creed. All that remains is one question: How to go about it?

It is the golden age of classification theory. We shall look briefly at a few classifications which this theory has produced.

Reader Interest Classification (RIC)

This idea is generally associated with Ruth Rutzen and the Detroit Public Library branches, where it began in the early 1940's. In one form or another it is to be found in a number of public libraries; application of the idea may vary greatly from library to library. What follows is based on Miss Rutzen's account of the Detroit Public Library system presented at a University of Illinois Allerton Institute held November 1–4, 1959 (Eaton, p.53–61).

RIC centers not on shelving books nor on logic, but on people and the fields of interest related to the everyday needs of people. These fields of interest arise from people's concern about themselves as (1) individuals, (2) members of a family, and (3) members of the local, national, and international community. To serve these fields of interest, books are arranged in two kinds of categories: browsing and subject.

Browsing categories are to serve "(1) the readers who have no fixed needs in mind but who are stimulated to recognize their interests by the category indicating a broad general field; and (2) those who are conscious of their interest in certain fields and can associate it with definite subjects but not with related interests."

Subject categories are to serve "the reader who comes to the library for help with a particular need but not necessarily a specific request. In large part the practical books concerning family life, vocational and avocational subjects fall here."

In 1959, Detroit was using fourteen categories: Background Reading, the Arts, Current Affairs, People and Places, the Bright Side, Sports, Hobbies, Personal Living, Your Family, Your Home, Group Activities, Business, Technology, Information. A category may have several subheadings.

Notation is simple. Each category is assigned a letter, each subheading a numeral: e.g., C2 would stand for Current Affairs—International Affairs; G2 for Your Home—Entertaining. Under each subheading books are arranged alphabetically. The cataloging is like that for any book except for the category-and-subheading call number. Assignment of category and subheading to a book is done at the branch. Regular reference books receive ordinary DDC call numbers.

All this amounts to broad classification rather than close (as in DDC and LCC), with an attempt to bring together related topics which might be separated in DDC. Thus the problem of the book with more than one subject is, perhaps, not quite so acute. But, like DDC and LCC, RIC adapts to change only by changing the call numbers. Presumably there would be considerable movement of books into and out of the collection anyway in order to keep it up to date.

With regard to the focus on "reader interest," no classification will say that it is not useful to the reader. Indeed, we have seen that Sayers and Merrill insist that usefulness is a basic consideration. On the other hand, with RIC, as with the conventional schemes, there is no scientific demonstration that the result is actually as useful as is claimed. Indeed, there are only general and subjective opinions of public service people based on their interpretation of their experience with the scheme.

The precise meaning of the names of the categories is not immediately obvious. How would the reader know the difference between "Your Home," "Your Family," and "Personal Living"? Would he look under "Information" or under a more specific subject? Would the reader guess that "Poetry" is under "Information"? The scheme itself has directions for the use of people assigning categories and subdivisions, but these directions are unknown to the reader. Presumably definitions might be added to the shelf labels, but would the reader bother to read them?

To what extent this classification brings together under categories books which in DDC would be scattered may be seen from the "Sample Selection of Shelf List" giving DDC call numbers as well as category-plus-subdivision for each title. (This "Sample Selection" is an appendix to a pamphlet, *The Reader Interest Book Arrangement in the Detroit Public Library*, distributed by Miss Rutzen to the audience when she presented her Allerton paper.) Summaries of four sheets chosen at random from these shelf lists follow:

YOUR FAMILY—CHILD CARE

24 books with 8 DDC call numbers:
1 book in 000's

18 in 100's including $\begin{cases} 9 \text{ at } 173.6 \\ 7 \text{ at } 150.2 \\ 2 \text{ at } 173 \end{cases}$

4 in 300's including 2 at 371.74
1 in 600's

CURRENT AFFAIRS—TRENDS IN SCIENCE

17 books with 10 DDC call numbers:
1 book in 300's

6 in 500's including $\begin{cases} 3 \text{ at } 500 \\ 2 \text{ at } 530.1 \end{cases}$

10 in 600's including $\begin{cases} 4 \text{ at } 629.258 \\ 2 \text{ at } 621.81 \end{cases}$

PEOPLE AND PLACES—ADVENTURE

25 books with 15 call numbers:

3 books in 500's including

2 at 591.92

1 in 600's

1 in 700's

15 in 900's including $\begin{cases} 3 \text{ at } 910.4 \\ 2 \text{ at } 917.98 \\ 3 \text{ at } 919.9 \end{cases}$

5 in B

THE BRIGHT SIDE

25 books with 5 call numbers:

15 books in 800's including $\begin{cases} 4 \text{ at } 818 \\ 11 \text{ at } 808.7 \end{cases}$

6 in F

1 in 900's

3 in B

To the extent that these four sheets are typical, it would seem that in each category there is a relatively small number of different call numbers, a not inconsiderable number of books with the same DDC call number, and a relatively large number of books in one of DDC's major classes. Perhaps in a small collection many of the books in a category might be fairly close together anyway. (It might be interesting to see what would happen if books on display in a browsing collection were shelved by their DDC call numbers but with striking labels explaining the meaning of broad classes or subclasses of DDC.)

Perhaps major problems with RIC would be administration and cost. Choice of categories and assignment of specific books to categories and subheadings are done in the Detroit branches. This practice means a lack of standardization; copies of the same book may have different call numbers in different branches. It also means that each book receives both a DDC call number and a RIC call number. In effect, this means reclassification when a book is added to the RIC collection and again when the book is returned to the regular DDC collection.

The central idea of RIC is intriguing. Whether it does, indeed, achieve its goal and how much more expensive it is than conventional DDC or LCC, we do not yet know.

The Bibliographic Classification (BC)

Henry Evelyn Bliss believed that a functional bibliographic classification should be consistent with the structural organization of knowledge representing the consensus of scientists and educators. This idea of consensus is central to his Bibliographic Classification (BC); and in practice, it would seem to mean a sort of reader interest classification for scholars.

BC was published in four volumes, 1940–53. It was the culmination of many years of study, articles in library journals, and three thoughtful books: *Organization of Knowledge and the System of the Sciences*

(1929), *Organization of Knowledge in Libraries and the Subject Approach to Books* (1933; 2d ed., 1939), and *A System of Bibliographic Classification* (1935). The first two were studies of the theory of classification; the last was a two-place expansion of the scheme which he had outlined in his *Organization of Knowledge in Libraries.*

Notation, Bliss felt, should not determine order, and it should be brief. The "economic limit" might be three or four factors in a call number, although close classification might require more. The letters of the alphabet mark the main subject classes. In addition to the letters there are nine Anterior Numeral Classes (used chiefly for form and special collections) and twenty-two Principal Systematic Auxiliary Tables performing functions much like those of the common "divide-like" subdivisions of DDC. Some of these tables are applicable throughout the scheme; most apply only to specific subject areas.

The BC notation reflects more than just the "consensus" idea; it also reflects Bliss's feeling that there should be "Gradation by Speciality" (i.e., movement from the fundamental to the more special) and "Collocation" (i.e., bringing together closely related subjects).

Gradation by speciality determines the order of the four main topics in BC's Concise Synopsis: Philosophy–Science–History–Technologies and Arts. In turn, gradation by speciality determines the sequence of the lettered classes which come out of these four main topics. Thus, Philosophy and General Science (A) is a fundamental group, and Physics (B) is somewhat more special. Physics, in turn, deals with the most fundamental of phenomena, the nature of matter and energy, and Chemistry (C) is somewhat more special than Physics because to some extent it draws on the findings of physicists. With D (Astronomy, Geology, Geography, and Natural History) and then with E (Biology), we move into a series of ever more special areas. Biology (E) is itself the containing science for Botany (F), Zoology (G), and Anthropology (H).

Collocation brings together languages and their literatures in the three philology main classes: non-Indo-European (W), Indo-European (X), and English (or other) language and literature (Y). If a technology is closely related to a science, the scheme brings them together. More general technologies are in class U (Useful Arts, etc.).

Alternative location is a third prominent feature of the notation. Psychology, for instance, is I, between Anthropology (H) and Education (J); but it may alternatively be put in AI with emphasis on its relation to metaphysics. X, we saw above, is for English *or other* language and literature, a concession to the language of the library. Although U contains primarily the useful and industrial arts, and the scientific technologies are collocated with their sciences in B–D, yet some of the latter may be alternatively placed in U. For literature (in W, X, and Y) the classifier may choose one of four different ways to treat the literary texts, as opposed to literary criticism, history, etc. These are only a few examples of alternative locations in the scheme.

BC is scholarly and it is carefully worked out. Class numbers are brief and the notation is quite expansible with alternative locations at many points. Finally, the scheme will probably be kept up to date by the British Committee for the Bliss Classification.

Yet BC is used in fewer than one hundred libraries; it is used almost not at all in the country of its birth. Perhaps the chief reason for this neglect is that Bliss came too late. Most American libraries use DDC or LCC; to change to even a perfect system would require time and money. Moreover, the printed card services generally provide DDC and/or LCC call numbers. Finally, there is the American feeling that call numbers are simply finding devices. A DDC or an LCC call number can find a book readily enough, why change?

There are at least two problems of logic:

1. Gradation by speciality and collocation (in the Bliss sense) are all very well perhaps with the minor subclasses of a subject; they may, indeed, be quite desirable, but in the main classes they are definitely a minor consideration. In a large research library, for instance, there is little gained by beginning with the very first book of A at the very first shelf in the bottom of the stacks and then moving in orderly sequence to the very last book of Z at the end of the very last shelf at the top of the stacks. Instead, classes of books—regardless of their sequence in the notation—tend to be shelved in whole or in part wherever seems to be the most useful location.

2. Alternative locations are, perhaps, good to have, but they mean tailor-made call numbers in every library. The classifier must spend more time deciding which variation to adopt. Even worse, if the time should ever come when it is desirable to print cards with BC call numbers (as is now done with LCC and/or DDC numbers), much more work would be necessary at the card-printing agency because in many cases at least two call numbers would have to be devised for a book.

If there truly is such a thing as a "consensus," why are there any —let alone many—alternative locations?

International Classification (IC)

Fremont Rider's International Classification (IC) was a latecomer to the American library classification scene (1961). In a vigorous introduction Rider insisted that his scheme is not to be used for reclassifying; "very seldom indeed . . . is the reclassification of a library worth what it costs." Rather, he hoped to interest brand-new libraries or libraries with no classification at all or old libraries "which may wish to maintain their classification status quo; but as of a certain date to classify their new acquisitions 'internationally'" (p.xi), that is, to use Ranganathan's osmosis idea.

Also this is a scheme, as he insisted in the full title of the book, "for the arrangement of books on the shelves of general libraries." The problem with DDC, LCC, and BC, he suggested, was a confusion of library classification with bibliographical classification. Bibliographical classification is needed for specialized fields and special libraries. It provides close classification for pamphlets, documents, articles, etc.; it is prepared by experts in the subject; and each bibliographical classification should be frequently revised. Library classification is needed for general libraries. It provides relatively broad classification for books; it is prepared by generalists; and each classification scheme need not be so frequently revised both for reasons of economy and because broad classification does not go out of date as rapidly as close classification.

"The First Edition of Dewey was . . . so amazingly simple and so amazingly practical that his enthusiastic disciples swallowed whole the entirely natural idea that, if some classification was good, more of it—in fact a great deal more of it—would be better" (p.xiii). Thus they forgot the difference between library classification and bibliographical classification; they rushed into the "Mediaeval Period of Dewey" with a "veritable rash of expansions in many of its schedules" through the fourteenth edition and a tendency to "divide like" to the longest possible call number (p.xiv). To some extent this was true also of LCC, and BC's Auxiliary Tables offer "a complexity beside which Dewey is simplicity personified" (p.xxiii).

In IC, Rider would correct the bias in DDC and LCC simply by making better provision for other countries, other cultures, and other religions; it would be a truly "international" scheme.

Notation, as in LCC and BC, is based on the alphabet. Every call number is exactly three letters long, and Rider points out that this gives a much larger base ($26 \times 26 \times 26 = 17{,}576$) than would DDC even if call numbers were restrained to four digits ($10 \times 10 \times 10 \times 10 = 10{,}000$). Three-letter call numbers, he estimates, would take care of a library of a million volumes, as opposed to three quarters of a million for four-digit call numbers. Although IC provides no more than three letters for any one call number, a library might, of course, expand any number it wished simply by adding another letter.

IC met the "divide like" problem head on; there are no "divide likes" whatever. Subdivision of any sort is built into the tables wherever practical (p.xxii).

On the whole, the sequence of main classes (and often the initial letters) is close to that of LCC. In detail, individual subject areas now and then come close to DDC. Relative importance is assigned to countries not on the basis of power or size but simply on the basis of printed matter published or apt to be published in or about them. The same is true of religions. Local history and geography are combined.

A few specific areas are noted below:

Although A (as in LCC) is a "Generalia" class, it begins with Book Arts, Bibliography, Libraries, and Rare Books, and only then gets to General Cyclopedias and the rest; that is, it looks in general like an LCC Class A preceded by LCC Class Z, or like DDC Class 000 with the parts switched around. Subject bibliography is scattered throughout the scheme.

Individual languages (X) are close to literature (Y: Literature. Europe. and Z: Literature. Rest of the World.). This, of course, differs from the separation of DDC 400 and 800; on the other hand, as in LCC, individual languages are generally separated from the corresponding literatures, e.g., XB: English language. and YB–YC. English literature. Individual literatures, unlike LCC and somewhat like DDC, are subdivided by form: Drama, Poetry, Fiction, and Miscellany. Miscellany, unlike DDC's definition, includes "any kind of literature whatever other than poetry, drama, and fiction."

For book numbers Rider uses the Biscoe Date Table to provide a number which arranges books with the same classification number first by date and then by author's name.

Thus IC may seem to offer a number of advantages over some of the schemes we have considered such as: shorter call numbers, a more "international" point of view, importance allotted to various countries on the basis of books actually concerned with them, merging of geography and local history, and book numbers which reflect chronology.

With IC, as with BC, the chances that many American libraries will adopt the new scheme are slim chiefly because of investment in DDC or LCC—and basic conservatism. Perhaps the function of a new classification scheme is much like the function of the new edition of an established scheme (e.g., DDC 17). It suggests solutions some of which libraries may want to adopt (and adapt!) to patch up holes in the schemes they are already using.

A new classification scheme bucks standardization and economy. It also reaffirms the inventive individualism without which there is no progress.

From Book to Microthought

Thus far we have talked of classification schemes from which we get call numbers to use as devices for shelving books in American general libraries. These schemes are generally based on a subject approach, but, speaking very broadly, we have not been too disturbed if they did not present a perfectly worked out system of knowledge provided they did, indeed, give us a cheap and efficient way to shelve books. Melvil Dewey himself (see p.99–100 above) laid down the law for us: "Detaild explanation of selection and arranjement of the many thousand heds wud be tedius; but everywhere filosofic theory and accuracy hav yielded to practical usefulness." For almost one hundred years we have followed the Master—even when we did not use his decimals.

Yet, even before Melvil, there were some who sought "filosofic theory and accuracy," and the search goes on today—abroad perhaps more than in America. Such a search may be better suited to the arrangement of entries in a classified catalog and to the attempt to locate not books so much as "microthoughts," i.e., the minute subjects or parts of a subject to be found in a pamphlet, periodical article, or part of a book. We shall look briefly at a few of these schemes.

Colon Classification (CC)

Although the Colon Classification (CC) is not widely used even in India, the country of its birth, much of the talk and thinking about classification in the past twenty-five years—particularly that outside America—has been derived from or inspired by CC's creator, S. R. Ranganathan. The first edition of CC was published in 1933, the sixth in 1960. Each edition has seen many changes, and Ranganathan has set forth in detail the development of the theory behind the system and its changes in a multitude of articles and books. Perhaps the most distinctive features of CC are faceted structure and notational synthesis. These terms are only a first step into the morass of jargon in which Ranganathan shrouds his ideas. In the following paragraphs something of what they seem to mean will be set forth.

(CC 6 consists of three parts bound in one volume: Part 1: Rules. Part 2: Schedules of Classification. Part 3: Schedules of Classics and Sacred Books with Special Names. Each part has its own pagination. References below are to Part number and page, e.g., 1.98 means Part 1, page 98. With a copy of the book in hand what follows may be somewhat easier to understand.)

Like traditional systems, CC begins with more or less traditional main classes for which the chief notation is the capital letters of the roman alphabet. But CC also uses lowercase roman letters, arabic numerals, and a few Greek letters, some capitals and some lowercase (2.4). Each main class may be divided "on the basis of one or more Trains of Characteristics" (1.20). A "facet" is the total subclasses resulting from one such division. Thus, in the class Literature "we may recognize four facets: The Language, The Form, The Author, and The Work" (1.20).

Here we meet what we have found to be the major problem in subject headings and in classification: What element comes first? The Cutter-Haykin subject heading would call for direct and specific entry of the specific subject. DDC calls for division of Literature by Language, then Form, then Period, then Author, then Work. LCC would have it Language, then (sometimes) Period, then Author, then Work. Each solution is claimed to be "useful"; each solution is arbitrary.

The CC solution is equally arbitrary. At the head of each class is listed the pertinent "Facet Formula" for that class. For O (Literature) the facet formula is Language, then Form, then Author, then Work. "Faceted structure," then, would seem to mean that each class is divided according to its facets and that the sequence in which facets appear in call numbers depends on the facet formula for that class. All of this may seem to be only a fancy way to describe what is often done anyway in DDC and LCC. We cannot say the same for notational synthesis.

Suppose the cataloger has a book of general literary criticism of Shakespeare. If he looks in the Index of DDC 16, he is directed to 822.33. The facets here and in DDC 17 are clear enough: Language (820: English), then Form (822: Drama), then Period (822.3: Elizabethan), then Author (822.33: Shakespeare). In DDC 16 a note refers the cataloger to a table for "arrangement of works by and about Shakespeare . . . at end of volume 2." In DDC 17 such a table immediately follows 822.33. With DDC he has, then, a ready-made call number and all he has to do is find it in the schedule.

The schedule of CC is much shorter. The cataloger gets his call number thus: He begins with O, the Literature class (1.98). He learns here that there are four facets referred to respectively as [P] Language, [P2] Form, [P3] Author, and [P4] Work. This is the facet formula of the class. Further, he is here told how to get the "Isolate Number" for each facet. ("Each division in a Facet is said to be an Isolate Focus (IF) or simply an Isolate (I)"—1.22; and "In the Plane of Notation, Isolate Number (IN) is the equivalent of Isolate Focus" —1.23.)

For the isolate number of the first facet—[P] Language—he is referred to 2.94, and here he is referred to the Language Divisions beginning 2.95. At 2.95 he finds that the number for Modern English is 111. Thus far he has a call number O111. It means: Literature—Modern English.

For [P2]—Form—he returns to 2.94 where he learns that 2 is the number for Drama. The call number is now O111,2. (At 1.5–1.6 he will have learned that the comma is one of eight "Connecting Symbols" which serve "only as connectives or conjunctions in the Colon language.") The call number now means: Literature—Modern English—Drama.

For [P3]—Author—he is referred to the "Chronological Device" with "Minimum of three digits" based on the year of birth of the author (although the scheme will allow him to choose to base this element on the author's name). In the "Time Isolate" Table (2.7) "J" is the letter for the period A.D. 1500 to 1599. To make "three digits" he adds 64. "J," that is to say, stands for the first two digits of the date of Shakespeare's birth: 1564. To make "three digits" he has added to "J" the last two digits of 1564, i.e., 64, thus producing J64 to represent the date of Shakespeare's birth, 1564. The call number is now O111,2,J64. It means: Literature—Modern English—Drama—Shakespeare.

For "Criticism" he will have read (1.16 and 1.17) that if a book is written about another book and is best kept with it, the original book is called the "Host Book" and the book about it is called the "Associated Book"; "the Book Number of an Associated Book should consist of that of its Host Book followed by ':g'." (The colon is, of course, another "Connecting Symbol.") The call number is now O111,2,J64:g. It means: Literature—Modern English—Drama—Shakespeare—Criticism.

If, however, English is the "Favoured Language" of his library, the call number would be simply O—,2,J64:g (see 1.54). This produces economy of notation and also shelves books in the favored language ahead of those in other languages.

So with CC the cataloger has no ready-made call number; instead he works out a "piece" of a call number to stand for each element in the subject and then he brings the pieces together. This approach may be able to bring out aspects the maker of the scheme might never dream of; in an "enumerative" scheme such as DDC there are only the numbers which the maker has thought out. Also it may be possible to produce close classification numbers more easily. Ranganathan, however, intended CC 6 only for classifying "Macro Thought embodied in books . . . in general libraries"; for the "Depth Classification of Micro Thought" he intends to publish "depth schedules" as "separate fasicules" (Preface, p.10–11).

Very briefly we shall look at three other features of CC: the "Fundamental Categories," the "Rounds and Levels of Manifestation," and the "Octave Device."

CC maintains that in the analysis of a subject each facet is a manifestation of one of five "Fundamental Categories"; they are listed below in what CC calls "the increasing sequence of concreteness" (1.25–1.26).

With each is also listed its "Connecting Symbol" and the initialism symbol for the facet which manifests the category.

FUNDAMENTAL CATEGORY (FC)	CONNECTING SYMBOL (CS)	SYMBOL FOR THE FACET
Time	. (Dot)	[T]
Space	. (Dot)	[S]
Energy	: (Colon)	[E]
Matter	; (Semicolon)	[M]
Personality	, (Comma)	[P]

Probably these five "Fundamental Categories" are better known in the decreasing "sequence of concreteness": Personality, Matter, Energy, Space, Time,—or simply PMEST. Of the five, "Personality" is probably the most difficult to define. In the first three editions of CC, the colon was the only connecting symbol; here it is used only with Energy, but Ranganathan feels that there is no need to change the name "Colon Classification" because Energy's "Manifestation alone can initiate Rounds of Manifestation" (1.28).

As to "Rounds of Manifestation," "Energy may manifest itself in one and the same subject more than once," and these successive "Manifestations" are called "Second Round Energy" [2E], "Third Round Energy" [3E], etc. In addition, there may be "Manifestations" of "Personality" and "Matter" after the "First Round Energy"; these are called "Second Round Personality" [2P] and "Second Round Matter" [2M]; and so on (1.27).

By way of example, CC (1.27) suggests L:4:616;41171 (Cure of disease by saline injection), which may be analyzed as follows:

L	Medicine			(1.88)
:4	Disease	[E]	(Problem facet)	(2.83)
:616	Injection	[2E]	*cum* [2P]	(2.85)
;41171	Salt	[3M]		(2.47)

As to "Levels of Manifestation," "In each round there may be more than one manifestation of Personality and Matter" (1.28). These are called "Second Level Personality" [P2], "Third Level Personality" [P3], "Second Level Matter" [M2], and so on. (You remember that the four facets of Literature were listed as [P] Language, [P2] Form, [P3] Author, and [P4] Work.)

The "Octave Device" (1.5–1.6) provides that in notation the following numbers are coordinate although they have a different number of digits in them: 1, 2, 3, 4, 5, 6, 7, 8, 91, 92, 93, etc., through 98, 991, 992, 993, etc., through 998, etc. This allows an indefinite number of coordinate subdivisions instead of (as in DDC) only 9. In the same way, "z" and "Z" may be used as "Octavising" digits.

These are only a few of the almost infinite variety of ingenious devices in CC. The facet idea, we have noted, is not new, although Ranganathan did give it a name and for the first time tried to apply it consistently. Whether it is useful enough to the reader to deserve this much attention remains to be proved. Notational synthesis allows a much shorter printed schedule than if the scheme listed every combination its maker could think of; on the other hand, it frees the classifier to invent combinations the maker might never have thought of. Yet notational synthesis is also not entirely new; compare the "divide like" tables in DDC and LCC. Finally, synthesis demands more time than ready-made numbers.

There is unconscious irony in P. N. Kaula's praise of CC when he states that the scheme's "outstanding contribution" is the concept of "Facet-Analysis" and that "the days of the enumerative pattern" are gone; for he then at once suggests that CC does need a "schedule and an index of ready-made class numbers" so that semi-professionals or non-professionals could apply the scheme in smaller libraries. These two features, he thinks, explain the popularity of DDC "in spite of its outmoded enumerative pattern and several defects" (*Library Science Today; Ranganathan Festschrift* [1965], p.92).

The "Fundamental Categories" and the "Manifestations" seem like an overly elaborate statement of a few basic facts. Moreover, how do we know that there are only five "Fundamental Categories"? We may have here an arbitrary assumption as restrictive as Dewey's tens. The sequence of the "Connecting Symbols" or of the Greek letters scattered among the Roman also would surely seem arbitrary to the user in open stacks. The "Octave Device" is most ingenious, but to insist that anyone would ever guess that 8 is the same kind of number as 9991 in notation is to go against common sense. Surely this again must seem quite arbitrary to the user.

Perhaps the chief problem with CC is communication. In order to get anything like consistency among libraries—or even among workers in the same library—the scheme would need more specific and clearer instructions. CC too often takes common terms (such as "Facet," "Personality," or "Manifestation") or common usages (such as punctuation marks or arabic numeral sequence) and gives them new and different, quite technical meanings. CC piles sin onto sin when it then insists on referring to these terms only by initialisms. A classification scheme, like many another part of life, can be used only if it can be easily understood. It has a chance of being understood only if it really tries always to be clear and simple.

Universal Decimal Classification (UDC)

Unlike the other schemes we have discussed, the Universal Decimal Classification (UDC) is not an original invention. Instead it is a hybrid.

UDC began in the late nineteenth century with permission to modify and expand DDC for use in constructing a huge classified index to all publications. The sponsor was the newly formed Institut International de Bibliographie, now known as the Federation International de Documentation (FID), and the guiding spirits were Paul Otlet and Henri La Fontaine. The index idea was later abandoned, but over the years FID and devoted editors have developed the schedule into a vast and complicated system for detailed specification of information. That is, UDC is basically a scheme for microthought. Various editions of UDC have appeared in whole or abridged versions or in sections, and in various languages. There is also the helpful *Guide to the Universal Decimal Classification* (1963).

UDC is a "universal" classification in that it tries to cover all knowledge and also in that it tries to be truly international, backed as it is by an international organization. It follows in many respects the basic organization of DDC, although there have been major adjustments. At the same time, UDC, like CC, has increasingly sought to develop a faceted approach and notational synthesis. The basic notation is, of course, arabic numerals used decimally, but without the three-digit minimum of DDC. Thus DDC's 500 (Science) and 540 (Chemistry) became simply 5 and 54 respectively. The period is placed after every three digits, e.g., 543.361.3.

Facets are represented in UDC in two ways:

1. Simple enumeration such as occurs in DDC. For example, 8 is the number for Literature and numbers 82 through 89 are devoted to the Language facet. Thus, 87 is Classical literature, and 882, Russian literature.
2. "Auxiliaries," usually preceded by special symbols or "facet indicators." There are two kinds of "auxiliaries":

   A "common auxiliary" may be used as a facet of any class if need be. Perhaps the best-known common auxiliary is that introduced by a colon. For instance, "Studies of admission to grammar schools" might be 373.51:371.212. In this compound 373.51 is grammar schools and 371.212 is admission. (Strictly speaking, the colon in this case may be said to introduce a subordinate concept only if there is no duplicate entry: 371.212:373.51.)

   A "special auxiliary" is special to the class to which it belongs. For instance, in 8 (Literature) a 7 introduced by a facet indicator .0 (i.e., .07) may be used as an alternative to 4 to indicate linguistic studies. Russian philology thus becomes 882.07.

There are some fourteen auxiliaries for such things as: addition of numbers both consecutive and nonconsecutive; relation of subjects (e.g., the colon above); language; form; place; race and nationality; time; point of view; and so on. In addition, there may be alphabetical or numerical non-UDC subdivisions, e.g., 92(Wells) for a life of H. G. Wells. All this, of course, allows considerable diversity, but it also requires rather arbitrary filing rules for the "facet indicators." The auxiliaries will be recognized as extensions of the "divide likes" and the "common subdivisions" of DDC.

Perhaps the major achievement of UDC is that it can specify almost any subject. It does this with detailed enumeration of subdivisions and with the "auxiliary" apparatus. This means that the numbers may be quite long.

Also there is the problem of DDC. UDC has departed radically from DDC, but it retains the same basic approach and the same basic separation of the various aspects—e.g., economic, business administration, engineering, legal, and so on—of a subject. This is the way with a general classification such as DDC; it would seem to be awkward in a special library. To some extent the auxiliaries help get away from this. At the end of the *Guide to the Universal Decimal Classification* (1963), there is a thirteen-page list of a "small selection of the many thousands of libraries and documentation centres that use the UDC," but only a handful are described as "General Scope (National and University Libraries, etc.)."

UDC shares a miracle with its noted parent: It is preposterous but it works.

Where Does the Book Go?

The possibilities are infinite, ranging from fixed location to Colon. In an American general library, a call number is only a shelving device, and it almost always is based on DDC or LCC. If possible, the cataloger takes it from a printed card for the book. Or the call number may simply shelve by fixed location. We know, of course, that none of the three is perfect. But we also know that the search for perfection lasts forever and that our time and energy do not.

7

Mr. Cutter's Catalog:
Today and Tomorrow

We have examined in some detail American cataloging theory and principles with respect to (1) author and title entry, (2) description, (3) subject headings, and (4) classification. Cutter's rules are the broad basis for treatment of all four elements except classification; even in classification Cutter's EC influenced LCC. What has happened in American cataloging since Cutter, has involved the interaction of (1) Rules and Classifications, (2) Duality of the Two Objectives, and (3) the Public as catalogers think of it. We shall summarize this interaction and the resulting dilemma.

Rules and Classification

Rules for author and title entry and for description developed after Cutter differ from Cutter in several ways: For instance, there was specialization and, sometimes, fragmentation. ALA 1908, ALA 1941, and ALA 1949 abandoned subject headings, smaller and nonscholarly libraries, special materials, and (perhaps most important of all) a statement of principles such as Cutter's "Objects." In addition, ALA 1949 abandoned description to LC 1949. ALA 1967 reunited author and title entry and description and included treatment of special materials.

Cooperation with the British appeared for the first time in ALA 1908; indeed, it was so marked that the code itself has the conventional title "Anglo-American Code." Because of the disruption of the Second World War, ALA 1941 and ALA 1949 were entirely American. LC 1949 was entirely LC, although ALA adopted it. ALA 1967 called itself "Anglo-American," but this was pertinent only for most of the rules for author and title entry. Rules for description and for special materials were simply LC rules with some ALA-LA revision.

Rules after Cutter tended to become more legalistic and more detailed. ALA 1941 was the high-water mark and produced Osborn's only partially successful revolution, which we still sometimes call "the crisis in cataloging." Perhaps the problem was that, as noted above, the ALA rules had abandoned Cutter's "Objects" although they retained with approval his statement on the paramount importance of the "convenience of the public." In any event, LC 1949 began with a statement of principles and was a rather coherently developed set of rules; on the other hand, ALA 1949 was simply a rehash of the detail of ALA 1941. Lubetzky 1960 leaned heavily on Cutter's "Objects," and Paris 1961 was based on Lubetzky 1960. In ALA 1967 the rules for author and title entry were rather coherently (if elaborately) developed about the principles of Paris 1961; the rules for description included the LC 1949 statement of principles.

The treatment of subject headings has changed little since Cutter. After him there was only one code, the Vatican, and this in large measure rests on Cutter's ideas. Haykin tried to explain LC use of Cutter's rules; but his book is simply a rationalization of the ever lengthening list of individual subject headings applied over the years by a series of LC subject catalogers, each trying to find what would best suit the "convenience of the public."

Classification, beginning with Dewey, has taken little account of theory and principles: instead, it has sought a practical book-shelving device which would best suit the "convenience of the public." DDC has suffered from the long conflict between the theoretical notion of "keeping pace with knowledge" and the practical convenience of "integrity of numbers." Until the present, LCC has been free from these slogans because it has remained a "private" classification scheme developed to serve its own need only. But if the trend away from DDC to LCC continues, LCC may well be dragged into the fray.

Duality of the Two Objectives

Entry, description, subject headings, and classification—each of these four basic elements involves a duality like that in Cutter's "Objects," which, following Lubetzky 1960, we call the two objectives. With each element we try to locate a book (1) as an entity and (2) as part of a group. Thus:

> Author and title entries locate in the catalog (1) a single book by a particular author and (2) all the books of a particular author together.
> Description locates in the catalog (1) a particular edition of a book and (2) all editions, issues, etc., of a book together.
> Subject headings locate in the catalog (1) a book on a particular

subject and (2) all books on the same subject together.

Classification locates on the shelves (1) a book on a particular subject and (2) all books on the same subject together.

Within each of these four pairs, the second objective causes trouble in at least three ways:

1. It does not completely serve its purpose. With author and title entry and with description, it does not bring together in the catalog all the works of an author and all the editions of a work if some have appeared in unanalyzed anthologies or collections. With subject headings and with classification, it brings together only material issued in separate books on a particular subject. It does not include books on a broader subject which may have as one of its elements the particular subject being sought.

2. It demands uniformity. The second objective can be attained only with: (a) uniform heading for an author no matter how his name may appear in a particular book; (b) uniform title for the various editions of a book even though different editions may appear under different titles; (c) uniform heading for a subject no matter what a particular book on that subject may call it; and (d) uniform call number for all books on a subject no matter what the books may individually call the subject.

3. Perhaps most important of all: (a) The cataloger sometimes finds it hard to identify and maintain the uniform element and make adequate cross references to it. (b) The user may not easily find under the uniform element what he seeks even if there are adequate cross references.

At this point the cataloger drops the two objectives and falls back on Cutter's doctrine of the "convenience of the public," and he does whatever he guesses will best serve that convenience.

The Public

We begin again with Cutter's famous paragraph (p.6):

> The convenience of the public is always to be set before the ease of the cataloger. In most cases they coincide. A plain rule without exceptions is not only easy for us to carry out, but easy for the public to understand and work by. But strict consistency in a rule and uniformity in its application sometimes lead to practices which clash with the public's habitual way of looking at things. When these habits are general and deeply rooted, it is unwise for the cataloger to ignore them, even if they demand a sacrifice of logic and simplicity.

We have seen that codes after Cutter abandoned his statement of objects for almost fifty years; while the "convenience of the public" was picked up almost at once and has served ever since as a sort of object to end all objects. On the one hand, it has a noble ring; who can deny that libraries exist to serve? One would as soon attack mother love or home. On the other hand, it is convenient; it gives us an excuse to do almost anything in the catalog.

Yet there is Marie Louise Prevost's classic question (*Library Quarterly*, 16:140 [1946]): "What is the 'public' which we, in general libraries, serve through the catalog? Children, young people, adults; the expert, the inept, the illiterate, the savant; scientists, artists, authors, teachers, and—librarians. Once the diverse nature of the users of the catalog is recognized, it becomes a patent absurdity to speak of cataloging according to the 'public' mind as if that mind were a single entity."

John Rather, for instance, once listed the "tradition-bound demands on the catalog" which had appeared time and again in the almost fifty articles written before 1955 by noncatalogers (*Journal of Cataloging and Classification*, 11:175–79 [1955]). Library administrators want to save money in the catalog. Public service librarians want the catalog to be simple and self-explanatory. Reference workers want the catalog to give all the answers to many questions, e.g., Winifred Ver Nooy and the detailed biography of R. R. Bowker which she once constructed using only catalog cards (W. M. Randall, ed., *Acquisition and Cataloging of Books* [1940], p.313–20). These are, indeed, contradictory demands, and they would result in different kinds of catalogs.

"Who is the public?" Many people have not been daunted by the question. They have tried to squeeze the answer from all sorts of things. They have studied soiled catalog cards, and they have indulged in the more sophisticated techniques of sampling and questionnaires and interviews. They have tried university users at one time, public library users at another—and they have tried all kinds of users at one time. Their answers have ranged from average age and average sex of the user to his average chance at success in getting something out of the catalog. (See Carlyle Frarey's perceptive summary of attempts to find the user in Maurice F. Tauber's *Subject Analysis of Library Materials* [1953] p.147–66). More ambitious than any study listed by Frarey was the *Catalog Use Study* by Sidney Jackson, edited by Vaclav Mostecky (1958). There were 5494 interviews with patrons in thirty-nine libraries ranging from large university libraries to high school libraries. Findings were extensive, but, on the whole, they did not differ greatly from those reported by Frarey. Moreover, in all studies to date the methodology leaves much to be desired and thus brings into question even such tentative conclusions as the studies may suggest.

"What is the public?" Miss Prevost's question remains. Is there such a creature as "the public," or are there many publics, each with its individual varieties and needs? Studies will, no doubt, continue as long as cash can be found to pay for them. Suppose some study were to succeed; suppose it were to show that there is only one user and to identify that user and his needs and habits. Would we dare to build a catalog around those habits and needs? Perhaps not. Habits and needs change; this year's man will not be the same man next year. A catalog built on this year's public's habits and needs might hinder next year's public. We might need an indefinite number of studies continued for an indefinite period of time, each study to be reflected in a new and different catalog to answer new and different needs.

Miss Prevost had her own answer to the convenience of the public (p.141–42):

> The only way to produce a clear theory is to cast loose all ties with the past for the time being; to analyze our objectives and our practices; and then to reconstitute. And in this reconstitution of the catalog it seems clear to me that our aim must be to make it a simpler tool for the librarian and, with a modicum of initiation, for the intelligent reader. The less intelligent must lean on professional competence— as, in fact, they always have done. In other words, we must make plain the truth that no one can use a catalog who does not know how, and, for those who do know how, we must make its use quicker, easier, and more sure, disavowing openly and without shame the pretense that it can be, successfully, a free-for-all.

Now the two objectives themselves arise from what we consider the primary convenience of the public. The two objectives thus become the basis of our bibliographical system. Yet, that system never becomes a truly, logically, and fully developed system because whenever the going gets rough we turn aside to Cutter's notion that we must follow the convenience of the public regardless of what that presumed convenience may do to the convenience of the bibliographical system. But a system is convenient only as long as it is a system.

Dilemma

The two objectives combined with convenience of the public make cataloging difficult to do and catalogs difficult to use. They do not produce identical answers for the same book in the hands of two catalogers. They do not produce identical answers in the minds of two users trying to find an entry for the same book. The plain fact is that two *different* answers for the same book may sometimes be equally logical and/or almost always equally conform to what may be defended as the convenience of the public. At this point, if LC has an answer we take it—perhaps in desperation.

Cataloging U.S.A. thus rests on three bases:

1. Cutter's "Objects"—our bibliographical system to the extent that we have one.
2. What is assumed (but never proved) to be the public's needs and/or wants. (They are not necessarily the same.)
3. Custom. Much more than we should like to admit, cataloging is only the accumulation of what has been done. Specifically, cataloging U.S.A. is the accumulation of what has been done in LC.

> The grizzly bear is huge and wild;
> He has devoured the infant child.
> The infant child is not aware
> It has been eaten by the bear.
>
> A. E. Housman

Dilemma—Parallel?

The situation may be desperate; it may not be unusual.

Cataloging practice may be, after all, a sort of language, the language of bibliographical description. Any language is to some extent the product of logic, or at least what may be explained in terms of what seems to be logic. But to a very large extent language seems to be the product of what the user of that language needs or wants for everyday conversation, and of custom, as established by the printed work of authors, particularly the printed work of noted authors. Dictionaries of a language draw on all three sources. Perhaps codes for cataloging are not entirely unlike language dictionaries in this respect.

Language is a tool for communication; it is a good tool to the extent that it is widely understood. Language is understood if it is standard; it need not always be logical (witness our own Melvil Dewey's adventure with simplified spelling). Nor need it be absolutely standard; consider the many differences in the English language as it is used by people in different parts of this country and abroad. Finally, two *different* words or phrases may be equally logical and/or convenient to the public for a particular circumstance.

Thus far we have looked at cataloging chiefly in terms of the three-sided conflict (some may call it cooperation) between the logic of the two objectives, the convenience of the public, and LC practice. If we assume that cataloging is, indeed, the language of bibliographical description, what are we to say of standardization in that language?

Standardization in cataloging U.S.A., past, present, and future, comes from many sources. We shall look at five: (1) Jewett, (2) Library of Congress, (3) Centralized and/or Commercial Processing, (4) The Machine, and (5) The Book Catalog.

Jewett

Many different catalogers in many different libraries catalog different copies of the same book. This has been true since Gutenberg. How can this duplication of work be avoided? For over a hundred years catalogers have looked for an answer. In the nineteenth-century book catalog the problem was even greater. After a library had published a catalog, the library could record its accessions in a card file and then eventually publish the file as a supplement to the catalog; but too many supplements would exhaust the user's patience. A new edition, incorporating the first edition and the supplements, was the obvious answer. But this meant that the library must have type set to relist not only the new books, but also the very same books it had listed before in the first printed catalog.

It was this problem that Charles C. Jewett sought to answer when he proposed (in 1853) the preparation of a separate stereotype plate for each title cataloged by the Smithsonian Institution. These plates could be used again and again. A library which wanted to print a catalog of its collection could use the pertinent Smithsonian plates and would be charged only for assembly and distribution of these plates, the composition of plates for new titles, and the presswork. The library would not have to recatalog titles already cataloged by the Smithsonian, and it would not have to pay printers for composing these titles.

Jewett's plan included rules for cataloging and a notable remark: "Nothing, so far as can be avoided, should be left to the individual taste or judgment of the cataloger" (p.8). The solution proposed to avoid duplication of work then is standardization. Duplication can be avoided if we invite some outsider to catalog all books for all libraries —*but* we must accept this outsider's work, and we must make our own work conform to it. Thus the invited guest becomes at once the invited intruder. The solution to an economic problem had a profound social implication: It would freeze the development of cataloging theory and rules.

For various reasons Jewett's scheme collapsed, but he had stated clearly the obvious solution and its obvious problem. We have tangled with both ever since.

Library of Congress

Beginning in 1901, LC made its cards available to libraries wishing to buy them. These cards are, of course, prepared for the LC catalogs, and they are somewhat more elaborate than many libraries feel they need. Since 1930 an LC office has added DDC numbers to some cards. These are, of course, DDC numbers applied with the very best intentions, but applied in a vacuum. They may be somewhat more lengthy than some libraries feel they need, and they may now and then shelve a book where a particular library does not want it. Moreover, the LC addition of DDC numbers to LC cards has been somewhat erratic. In 1934 the annual average of LC titles receiving DDC numbers was 99 percent, but beginning in the 1940's this steadily declined to 26 percent in 1964 (Verner Clapp in *Library Resources and Technical Services,* 9:393–413 [1965]). Since 1965 the number of LC cards with DDC numbers has tended to increase.

In the late fifties, with the help of a grant from the Council on Library Resources, LC undertook its most ambitious experiment in this area: cataloging-in-source. Briefly, the idea was to print on the reverse of each book's title leaf, or in some other convenient place, a copy of the LC card for that book. Cataloging would be done from page proof just before the book went to press. LC cataloged 1203 titles in this way and supervised a consumer reaction survey by a team headed by Esther Piercy. The LC report of what happened, *The Cataloging-in-Source Experiment* (1960), is an amazing document. On the one hand, the libraries surveyed were enthusiastic about the possibilities, although they were not unanimous about precisely how they would use the cataloging information or, indeed, how much of this information they really needed. On the other hand, LC found the experiment only a costly nuisance and stated flatly that there should be no further experimentation with the idea.

Perhaps the problem was perfectionism. At one blow we tried to get a complete and perfect card printed in every book. This meant that each book came to LC as an emergency. The catalog entry was the last thing done before the book could go to press; catalogers in Washington and publishers in New York had to be on their toes to meet publication deadlines. Even worse, last-minute changes in the publishers' offices now and then meant an error in collation, imprint, or even title transcription in the already finished entry. The "full card" idea, like every perfectionist idea, had lost sight of the real problem and made perfection its goal. Author headings, added entries, subject headings, call numbers—these are the costly items in cataloging. Every one of them could be added at any time after the publisher accepted the manuscript; indeed, the publisher could send them along with the manuscript to the printer. (This, of course, is simply an extension of what Ranganathan had called "Prenatal classification and cataloging of books"; see *Journal of Cataloging and Classification,* 12:21–22 [1956].)

The Cataloging and Classification Section of ALA asked the Librarian of Congress to consider a limited experiment of this nature, but the Librarian replied that LC was "in a position in which it is quite impossible for it to consider any additional projects" (*Library Resources and Technical Services*, 4:284 [1960]). The benefits to the library community would have been tremendous. At one end of the line, the publishers' catalogs, and all future catalogs of secondhand books, would have listed cataloging-in-source books under the same headings as they would later appear under in catalogs of libraries all over the country. At the other end of the line, even the tiniest one-man library would have ready-made cataloging which would need only someone to copy it. Standardization, complete and permanent.

With cataloging-in-source well out of the way, LC turned to substitutes. In late 1959, LC began to furnish *Publishers' Weekly* with (in addition to information previously given) DDC numbers and LC subject headings. In 1960 these entries began to go into Bowker's newly established *American Book Publishing Record* (*BPR*), and the LC report on cataloging-in-source suggested that this might be a good substitute for cataloging-in-source. But is it truly? LC catalogs a book and then separates the book from its LC entry; later in every library someone has to take time to try to find the entry in *BPR* or some other list and then connect the entry with the book again. Coverage is not an automatic and instant 100 percent as it would have been with cataloging-in-source. In September 1961, LC started the cards-with-books program working with such publishers and dealers as could be interested to enclose a packet of LC cards with each book sold; this, of course, is more like cataloging-in-source.

In the fall of 1963 the Association of Research Libraries (ARL) began informal discussion of their cataloging problem. They were spending about 16 percent of their total budgets on cataloging (some sixteen million dollars a year), and they had to do about 45 percent original cataloging of books for which LC cards were not available. Not surprisingly, backlogs had increased 160 percent in the previous decade. Most of the books for which LC cards were not available were current Western European publications.

ARL, ALA, and LC succeeded in getting written into the Higher Education Act of 1965 authorization for funds which LC would use in acquiring and providing cataloging information for, so far as possible, all library materials currently published throughout the world which are of value to scholarship. LC's John Cronin pushed ahead vigorously with plans in this country and abroad, working closely with foreign dealers and the authorities in each country responsible for that country's national bibliography. With adequate appropriations, the number of LC cards and the speed with which they become available should increase dramatically. (See *Library Resources and Technical Services*, 11:27–49 [1967].)

During the same period, with the assistance of the Council on Library Resources, LC began to study the possibility of recording and distributing cataloging data in machine-readable form. After some two years of study and discussion, the Machine-Readable Cataloging Project (MARC) resulted, with an initial planning phase beginning in 1966. Within two years a pilot system was designed and made operational, LC converted 35,000 records and distributed sixty-two tapes to sixteen participating libraries, an interim MARC system was designed and implemented to improve upon the first MARC system, a new format was designed, and programs and procedures were modified to process and distribute MARC II records on a subscription basis. (See the papers on MARC by Henriette D. Avram and others in *Library Resources and Technical Services*, 12:245–319 [1968].)

All this could lead to a national communications network in which machine-readable data could be transmitted electrically from library to library so that, as Verner Clapp suggested, "the catalogs that can be thus linked become one catalog and their libraries one library for the purposes of bibliographic access" (*Special Libraries*, 57:384 [1966]). The impact of MARC may be profound; the precise form this impact will take depends on LC's ultimate reaction to MARC, how libraries use it, and the possibility of getting continuing appropriations for it.

A novel development in LC's contribution to standardization came in November 1965. Mrs. Patricia S. Hines became head of a newly established LC Children's Literature Cataloging Section with responsibility for assuring cataloging coverage of currently issued children's literature and for adapting existing LC cards to assure coverage of earlier, in-print children's books. Modifications of standard LC practice on these cards included such things as a shortened DDC number, addition of a brief annotation, and some difference in the application of LC subject headings—e.g., use of fewer subdivisions—but very little difference in LC terminology (*Library Resources and Technical Services*, 10:455–60 [1966]).

Standard LC cards for these books also remained available. Thus, for the first time, LC's card publishing program began to affect standardization at two levels: that of the large scholarly library and that of a smaller, more specialized library.

Centralized and/or Commercial Processing

Apart from LC the drive toward standardization has come in recent years from centralized processing and commercial processing. Our concern here is only with the cataloging which each supplies. With centralized processing two or more libraries go together to do their cataloging and some or all of their other processing activities. The number of libraries involved, the particular services provided, where and how the work is done and managed—in these and other ways, there is great variation between processing centers.

Perhaps the oldest of the commercial services is the card service of H. W. Wilson Company; but many companies offering some or all cataloging and processing services have appeared in the last ten years or so. They differ from each other as much as the processing centers.

The standardization resulting from most centralized and/or commercial processing differs from that of LC and that of Wilson cards in at least one important way. LC cards are made for LC, not for the library of any purchaser of LC cards. They may have more elaborate description than some other library needs; their call numbers may be longer than some library needs; their call numbers may shelve books where that other library does not want them; or their subject headings may bring out more (or less) than the other library wants. Also, LC may change the ground rules at any time if it seems best to do so in the LC catalog. The "No Conflict" rule was such a change. Subject headings on LC cards change as LC subject headings change. Call numbers on LC cards change as DDC or LCC editions of (or even just additions to) the schedules change. A subscribing library may even find that now and then two editions of the same book get different call numbers or different sets of subject headings.

Wilson cards also offer little choice; indeed, they bring problems not unlike those of LC cards. The subject headings are from Sears; the call numbers are DDC; and the rules may now and then be changed.

With other centralized or commercial processing the subscribing library often has more choice. These cards are being made *for* the subscribing library. But this individual choice of detail is a choice which the subscribing library shares with several—sometimes many —other libraries. Generally, with both centralized and commercial processing a library may remain an independent minority and ask for special exceptions to the standard product. Apparently there are many such libraries (Sarah Vann in *Library Resources and Technical Services,* 10:461–78 [1966]; see also *Library Trends,* 16, No.1 [July 1967]). These variations are, of course, nothing new. For years individual libraries have changed LC or Wilson cards to meet what they considered their individual needs. Such independence, like all independence, has its price. The library has to set up its own standards and consult a shelf list, a name authority file, and a subject heading authority file before it can use the cards it has bought.

Just as LC cards and other projects push toward standardization in Cutter's "Full" cataloging, so commercial processing, the processing centers, and LC projects, such as that with cards for children's books, encourage (somewhat less rigidly) standardization in Cutter's "Medium" and "Short" cataloging. Thus convenience of the public as individuals becomes convenience of each of three groups of the public.

The Machine

The machine will be with us as long as men are lazy (we generally prefer the euphemism "efficient") and as long as men are inventive. The first condition will remain; the second may not be so certain. The cataloger and the machine are old companions; indeed, Gutenberg's machine created the cataloger, or at least the need for him. More recently the machine has freed the cataloger-scribe from handwritten cards, from duplicating his work many times, and from many another bit of donkey work. The machine has come far in recent years. Each month brings its flurry of articles and books and theories and counter-theories about what the machine can do and what it cannot do; to deal with them at all adequately, this book would have to become a fat serial. Here we shall try to talk only very generally about the machine and standardization in cataloging.

The machine imposes some conditions of its own. For instance, cataloging data must be in machine-readable form, and filing must be something the machine can do easily. Apart from the mechanical standardization of its limitations, the machine has generally been used to produce catalogs within the framework of our traditional standardization; this, for instance, seems to be true of much in the MARC project.

The first printed book looked like a manuscript. The first horseless carriage looked like just that: a horseless carriage. It is not impossible that eventually the machine will transform the catalog. For there is a magnificent variety in what the machine can do, ranging from turning out a title-a-line book catalog to recording more bits of information about a book than a card-catalog cataloger would ever hope to record. It can eliminate or change any type of entry from the centralized record the cataloger does not like. It may be that in the long run much more important than all the things the machine can do will be a side product, the answers to two questions: (1) Some things even the machine cannot do; which of these things do we really need? (2) The machine can do many things we could never do before; which of these things do we really need? The machine demands that we rethink our whole attitude toward our work. How will that affect standardization? Consider the book catalog.

The Book Catalog

The machine is notable, among other things, because it made

possible the return, after more than fifty years, of the book catalog.

In the forties came the printed catalog of LC cards and in the fifties the supplements each reflected some improvement which made it possible to get more entries onto a page and to make the entries somewhat easier to read. The first LC book catalog was an author catalog, and inevitably in the fifties came the other half, the LC subject catalog. Finally we had a printed catalog not merely of LC cards but of Union Catalog entries. The LC book catalogs were followed by many others, chiefly catalogs of large public library systems, notably among the first the Los Angeles County Public Library.

Whether the book catalog is cheaper than the card catalog we do not at present know; perhaps we shall never know because in comparing costs we are not comparing the costs of like things. There is a difference in service. Perhaps the chief advantage of the new book catalog over that of the nineteenth century is the speed of production. We can now have brand-new catalogs of an entire collection every year with regular supplements between the annual editions. We can supply complete, up-to-date catalogs in each branch of a system. The book catalog does not take as much room as a card catalog, and there can be as many copies as the library wants: in the main library, on various floors, in departmental libraries, in branches, even in the office of a college professor. Once again we have discovered how much easier it is to glance over many entries on a page than laboriously to thumb through a tray of cards.

The book catalog contributes to standardization as long as the catalog itself remains standard. But it has not always remained standard, and each deviation raises questions. We shall look briefly at a few.

LC began with book catalogs which simply reproduced the entries on LC cards, and a number of other book catalogs have followed this practice. But there are also book catalogs with briefer entries, some with title-a-line entries, some even giving only initials for authors' forenames. How much detail is really necessary in a catalog entry? Do we really need the two objectives in author heading?

LC began with an author catalog and later published a subject catalog; other book catalogs have had these and sometimes more divisions, e.g., a section for children's books. The divided catalog had already appeared in efforts to make a bulky card dictionary catalog more easily used; the book catalog reinforces this tendency. Do we need the dictionary catalog after all? Are the basic principles of a divided catalog the same as those of the dictionary catalog? Do we need to maintain the "unit card" approach, or shall we return to use of a true "main entry" idea as in the nineteenth-century book catalog? What of the nineteenth-century list-plus-index-or-indexes idea?

The tremendous investment of LC and the ARL libraries in their huge card catalogs froze "Institutions" and other curious things in ALA 1967. Will the frequent reproduction of entire catalogs in book form make possible true reform of catalog rules, at least for non-ARL libraries? Even in ARL libraries will it be possible to print the present catalogs as they stand, and then begin new catalogs for accessions constructed along different and better lines?

Standardization, we have suggested, is a sort of crutch needed by our bibliographical system because of the crippling effect of the convenience of the public. How long will it hold firm?

Cutter's Tomorrow

Cutter's "Objects," we have noted, offer the basis of a bibliographical system; but he insisted that the convenience of the public should not yield to the convenience of the bibliographical system. The user, however, is hard, if not impossible, to identify. He stands there only in shadowy outline as we try to psychoanalyze him. Consequently, we cannot construct a truly logical and orderly bibliographical system. All we can do is accumulate a set of practices.

At this point we suggested that cataloging is a bibliographical language and that, like any language, it is a good tool for communication to the extent that it is standard—not necessarily to the extent that it is strictly logical or even to the extent that it always fits the particular needs of individual users.

Then we examined a few of the aspects of standardization in cataloging with regard to Jewett, LC, centralized and commercial processing, and (to the quite limited extent which seems possible at this time) the machine and the book catalog. Here we found a sort of organized anarchy, a pinching legalism. To catalog a book or to find a book listed in a catalog, we need not know a general principle or even a rule; indeed, we often cannot find one if we try. We simply learn the practice. We learn it just as we learn a word or phrase in a foreign language. If we are in doubt there is always the "pony," the translation into practice in the catalogs produced by LC and the other makers of standardization.

"In the last two years," wrote Cutter in the Preface to the fourth edition of his *Rules*, "a great change has come upon the status of cataloging in the United States. The Library of Congress has begun furnishing its printed catalog cards on such liberal terms that any new library would be very foolish not to make its catalog mainly of them, and the older libraries find them a valuable assistance in the cataloging of their accessions, not so much because they are cheaper as because in the case of most libraries they are better than the library is likely to make for itself." Then, after some discussion of the possibility that an old library might want to change LC headings in some cases to conform to its own previous practice, he suggested that because of the trouble and danger of inconsistency in the catalog this might involve, "it would be well to adopt the Library of Congress rules unless there is some decided reason against them." The LC card of 1901 was, of course, a much simpler thing than the LC card of today with its sometimes fantastic elaboration of detail. But the basic ideas of today's LC card are still the basic ideas of Cutter's rules. It seems not impossible that Cutter would have the same advice today, at least for the ARL libraries.

There remain the other libraries. Here we have the standardized products of centralized and/or commercial processing and LC's special cards for children's books. These will accommodate Cutter's suggestion (p.11) that, in addition to the large library demanding "Full" cataloging, there are two other kinds of libraries requiring "Medium" and "Short" respectively.

The new book catalog is simply a return to a form of catalog with which Cutter began; thus far it has brought few, if any, basic changes in Cutter's ideas of what should be involved in a catalog. But the speed and ease with which the machine produces the new book catalog does seem to suggest that it may be possible to escape from the rigidity enforced by ARL libraries' investment in large card catalogs. Perhaps that would mean also escape from the convenience of the public to the convenience of the bibliographical system based on the two objectives. Meanwhile, however, standardization moves steadily in three directions: toward "Short," "Medium," and "Full." In each direction standardization seeks to conform to the convenience of the public or, at least, to the convenience of Cutter's three groups of that public.

Finally: The Cataloger's Tomorrow

"On seeing the great success of the Library of Congress cataloging, I doubted whether it was worth while to prepare and issue this fourth edition of my Rules; but I reflected that it would be a considerable time before all libraries would use the cards of that library, and a long time before the Library of Congress could furnish cards for all books . . . Still I cannot help thinking that the golden age of cataloging is over, and that the difficulties and discussions which have furnished an innocent pleasure to so many will interest them no more. Another lost art. But it will be all the better for the pockets of the public, or rather it will be better for other parts of the service—the children's room and the information desk, perhaps" (Cutter, p.5).

The "considerable time" has stretched into some three fourths of a century. The "golden age" was, indeed, over. Work on cataloging rules since Cutter has been that of the silver age, an age devoted only to endless elaboration of Cutter's work. And this time-eating elaboration, to some extent at least, may account for the failure to reach the day when LC "would furnish cards for all books."

But now we face standardization three ways: "Full," "Medium," and "Short"; with government funds, the Council on Library Resources, the profit motive, and the machine pushing one or more of the three. Perhaps Cutter's dream of "all cards" will come true, although, of course, not simply from LC cards or necessarily even from cards.

What of the cataloger? Will he then be free to give his talent to "other parts of the service"? Perhaps. There may very well gradually cease to be a demand for quantity, lots of catalogers in lots of big and little libraries. Standardization will do their work with printed cards and/or book catalogs and/or some as yet unspecified use of the machine.

But it seems possible that for a long time to come there will be a demand for quality. *Someone* will have to catalog each book at least once in LC and perhaps in some of the various processing centers and commercial processors. If that cataloger makes a mistake, the mistake will not simply lurk in his own library's catalog; instead, that mistake will go and pester anyone who is ever interested in that book any time, anywhere.

Quality will be imperative in another area, cataloging judgment. In a small library, for instance, which kind of service should the director buy? What kind of service should the public service librarians want? In the service the library does buy, what revisions, if any, will the public need? The library can get almost anything it wants if the library pays for it. Human nature being what it is, these choices may confront librarians for a long time to come. If librarians do not choose wisely, they may quickly begin to lose the money they save by not hiring a cataloger, or they may give less than adequate service. The need for catalogers may sharply decline; the need for library directors and library public service people to understand cataloging principles and uses may as sharply rise.

Proteus

Everything changes. This is not simply a flashy notion of an ancient Greek philosopher. It is a fact of everyday life. Change is a fact of cataloging. The cataloging centers and the machine are the latest change in cataloging. But they will not be the last. Tomorrow they may even be old fashioned.

Change is a fact in cataloging. But is it the substance of cataloging —or only the surface?

Index

Abbot, Ezra, 84
American Library Association
  Catalog Code Revision Committee, 16, 17–18
  Catalog Rules Committee, 9
  cataloging codes
    definition of "author," 24–26
    1908, xvii, 9–11, 24, 25, 32, 34, 41, 43, 52, 53, 55, 61, 138
    1941, xvii, 11–12, 24, 49, 52, 54, 55, 58, 61, 62, 138, 139
    1949, xvii, 14–15, 24–25, 26, 31, 33–37, 41–44, 138, 139
    1967, xviii, 17–19, 23, 25, 26, 31–37, 40–44, 49, 52–56, 58–63, 138, 139, 151
  on Decimal Classification Editorial Policy Committee, 110
  subject heading list, 83
Anglo-American Code, see American Library Association, cataloging codes: 1908, 1967
Anonymous works, headings for, 32–33
Association of Research Libraries, 18, 146, 151, 152
Author
  compiler as, 25, 26, 35
  corporate body as, 24–26, 30, 41–43
  definition of, 24–26
Author heading, 23–47
  books on, xvii–xix
  books whose authors change, 35–36
  books with more than one author, 34–35
  choice and form of name in, 27, 29, 30–31

form heading and, 43–44
"institution" in, 41–43, 95
non-author heading, 40–44
objectives, 27–28, 31–32, 139–40
pseudo-author heading, 41
serials, 36–40
uniform, 28–30

Bibliographic Classification, 126–28
Biscoe numbers, 123, 130
Bliss, Henry Evelyn, Bibliographic Classification, 126–28
Book catalogs, 149–51, 152
Book numbers, 122
  constructing, 123
  in International Classification, 130
Books
  on cataloging, xv–xxii
  classification, see Classification
  description, xvii–xix, 13, 48–64; objectives, 49–50, 53–55, 139–40
  location
    alternative, 127, 128
    fixed, 97–98, 115
    relative, 98, 102, 103, 112–13, 115
  reference, entry for, 35–36
  two-subject, 119–21
Brunet, Jacques-Charles, classification scheme, 104–5

Call numbers, 96–137
  change in, 108–11
  how to find, 116–22
  for monograph series, 116
  objectives, 96–97, 112–15
  for periodicals, 115–16

specific subject, 113
uniform, 96–97, 140
See also Notation
Catalog
   alphabetico-classed, 3
      subdivision in, 71, 72, 75
      subject entry in, 67–68
      subject heading treatment in, 84–
         87, 90
   book, 149–51, 152
   cards, 48–49; Library of Congress, 2,
      9, 11, 12, 110, 144–45, 146, 148,
      151–52
   dictionary, 3–4, 7–8, 69, 150
      subject entry in, 67, 68
   form, 1–3
   objects and means, 6–7
   printed, 2, 7–8; main entry in, 44–46
Cataloging
   author and title entry, 23–47
   books on, xv–xxii
   changes in, 151–53
   Cutter on, 2, 3, 5–8, 10–11
   descriptive, 13, 48–64
      objectives, 49–50, 53–55
      for serials, 62–63
   duplication in, 9, 144
   -in-source (Library of Congress), 145–
      46
   machine-readable, 147, 149
   objectives, 139–40, 142–43
   periodicals devoted to, xxi–xxii
   reclassification, 112
   standardization in, 143–53
Cataloging codes, xvii–xix
   ALA, *see* American Library Associa-
      tion: cataloging codes
   COSATI Standard, 19–20
   Cutter's, xvii, 5–8, 10–11, 27
   Jewett's, xvii, 4, 5
   Library of Congress, *see* Library of
      Congress: cataloging codes
   Lubetzky's, xviii, 15–17, 27–28, 31–
      35, 37, 41–44, 54–55, 139
   Panizzi's, xvii, 4, 43
   Paris 1961, xix, 17, 18, 28, 34, 37,
      40, 41, 43, 139
   Prussian Instructions, xviii, 11
   Ranganathan's, xviii, 91
   Vatican, xviii, 13–14, 139
Cataloging Rules and Principles (Lubet-
   zky), xviii, 15–16, 42
Classification, xx–xxi, 96–137
   bias in, 107–8
   Bibliographic, 126–28
   book, *vs.* classification of knowledge,
      103–6
   changes in, 108–11, 138–40
   close *vs.* broad, 113–15, 116, 118

Colon, 120, 131–35
criticism and interpretation, books on,
   xx–xxi
Dewey Decimal, *see* Dewey Decimal
   Classification
Expansive (Cutter), 100–101
finding call numbers, 116–22
   by form, 118
International, 128–30
Library of Congress, 101–3
   notation in, *see* Notation
objectives, 96–97, 140
periodicals on, xxi–xxii
problems, 123–24
Reader Interest, 124–26
reclassification, 112
   of serials, 115–16
   by subject, 118, 121
   of two-subject books, 119–21
Universal Decimal, 135–37
   See also Books: location
Classification of Books (Grace Kelley),
   xx, 114
Coates, E. J., on subject headings, xx,
   92–93
Code for Classifiers (Merrill), xx, 20–21,
   116–22
Collation, 57–61
Colon Classification (Ranganathan),
   119, 120, 131–35
Compiler as author, 25, 26, 35
Copyright, date of, 56
Corporate bodies
   as authors, 24–26, 30
      assembled by location, 95
      serials, 38–40
   institutions, entry under, 41–43
Crisis in Cataloging (Osborn), xviii,
   12–13, 42, 49
Cross references
   from classes to individuals, 80, 81
   Cutter on, 66
   eliminating duplicate entry, 78
   "see also," 80–81, 82
   to uniform element, 140
Cutter, Charles A., xvii, 1–8, 10–11, 23,
   36, 49, 55, 61, 65, 66, 138, 139
   on author entry, 27
   on compound subject headings, 70–
      71, 77, 87–88
   "convenience of the public," 7, 8,
      140–43
   on corporate authorship, 39
   definition of "author," 24
   on duplicate entry, 79
   Expansive Classification, 100–101
   on form entry, 94–95
   general code of, 5–8
   on imprints, 56

on Library of Congress cards, 151–52
on main entry, 44–45
on subject entry, 66–69
on subject heading subdivision, 71–73, 75, 76–77
syndetic approach, 80–81
on titles, 52, 53
on types of catalog, 84
Cutter–Sanborn numbers, 101, 123

Dates, in imprint, 56–57
Decimal Classification Editorial Policy Committee, 110
Detroit Public Library, Reader Interest Classification in, 124–26
Dewey, Melvil, 98–100, 101, 103–4, 106, 108–9, 131
Dewey Decimal Classification, xx, 21, 98–100, 101, 105, 116, 117, 139
bias in, 107–8
changes in, 108–10
classes, 103–4
close classification in, 113–14
compared to Library of Congress Classification, 102–3
introduction to, 122
notation, 106–7
and Universal Decimal Classification, 135–37
Documents, government, 115, 116

Edition, definition, 50
Entry
added, 44, 46
arbitrary, 33–44
defined, 23
main, 44–46
reasons for choice, 6
Expansive Classification (Cutter), 100–101

Government documents, classification, 115, 116
Guide to the Use of Dewey Decimal Classification, 21, 122

Haykin, David J., xx, 65, 139
on compound subject headings, 70, 71
on "see also" references, 80–81
on subdivision, 73–75, 77–78
Heading
anonymous works, 32–33
arbitrary, 33–34
author, see Author heading
definition, 27
form, 43–44, 94–95
for laws, 43–44
non-author, 32–47
non-subject, 94–95

pseudo-author, 41, 95
serial, 36–40
subject, see Subject heading
title, 32–33, 36–40, 45–46
uniform, 140
History
of cataloging, 1–5
subdivision by time in subject heading, 74–75

Illustrative matter, in collation, 57–58, 59
Impression, definition, 50–51
Imprint, 55–57
Index
to classification schemes, 117
to periodicals, 115
Institutions, heading for, 41–43, 95
International Classification, 128–30
Issue, definition, 51

Jewett, Charles C., 143
cataloging code, xvii, 4, 5
Smithsonian plate scheme, 144

Kelley, Grace O., Classification of Books, xx, 114

Laws, heading for, 43–44
Library of Congress
book catalogs, 150
book numbers, 123
cards, 2, 9, 11, 12, 146, 148, 151–52
Dewey numbers on, 110, 144–45
tracing on, 62
cataloging codes
1949, xvii, 14–15, 49, 52–56, 59, 60, 62, 63, 138, 139
Supplementary Rules, 49, 55
cataloging-in-source, 145–46
classification scheme, see Library of Congress Classification
editing of Dewey Decimal Classification, 110
and institution headings, 42
Machine-Readable Cataloging Project (MARC), 147, 149
"No Conflict" policy, 30–31
Studies of Descriptive Cataloging, xviii, 13, 49, 52, 54, 57, 58
subject heading list, 83, 117
subject heading practice, 77, 85
Library of Congress Classification, 101–3, 105, 117, 122, 139
bias in, 107–8
changes in, 108–11
close classification in, 113–14
notation, 107
Lubetzky, Seymour, xviii, 15–17, 18

on author entry, 27–28
cataloging code, *see* Cataloging codes: Lubetzky's
on uniform titles, 54–55

Machine-Readable Cataloging Project (MARC), 147, 149
Main entry, *see* Entry: main
Maltby, Arthur, xxi, 117–22
Merrill, William S., 117; *Code for Classifiers*, xx, 20–21, 116–22
Monograph series, call numbers for, 116

"No Conflict," 30–31
Notation, 106–7
in Bibliographic Classification, 127–28
in Colon Classification, 131–35
in Dewey Decimal Classification, 106–7
in International Classification, 129–30
in Library of Congress Classification, 107
pure and mixed, 107
in Reader Interest Classification, 124–25
in Universal Decimal Classification, 136–37
Notes, in description, 61–62

Osborn, Andrew D., *Crisis in Cataloging*, xviii, 12–13, 42, 49

Pagination, statement of, 58
Panizzi, *Sir* Anthony, cataloging code, xvii, 4, 43
Paris Statement, xix, 17, 18, 28, 34, 37, 40, 41, 43, 139
Periodicals
classification, 115–16
journals on, xxii
See also Serials
Persons, subject heading subdivision by, 75–76
Phase analysis, in classification of two-subject books, 119–21
Place
of publication, in imprint, 56
subject heading subdivision by, 76–78
Prevost, Marie Louise
on convenience of the public, 141–42
noun approach to subject headings, xix, 88–90
Printing, definition, 50–51
Processing, centralized and/or commercial, 147–49
Prussian Instructions, xviii, 11
Pseudo-author headings, 41, 95

Publication
date of, 56–57
place of, 56
Publisher, in imprint transcription, 56

Ranganathan, S. R., xviii
Colon Classification, 119, 120, 131–35
categories, 91, 133–34
Reader Interest Classification, 124–26
Reference works, entry, 35–36
Religious works, uniform headings for, 44
Rider, Fremont, International Classification, 128–30
Rules for a Dictionary Catalog (Cutter), xvii, 1–8, 65, 66–69
Rutzen, Ruth, Reader Interest Classification, 124–26

Sayers, W. C. Berwick, xxi; rules for classification, 117–22
Schwartz, Jacob, noun approach to subject headings, 87–88, 89, 90
Sear's *List of Subject Headings*, xix, 20, 83, 117
Serials
classification, 115–16
definition, 36
description, 62–63
entry for, 36–40
journals on, xxii
Series
kinds of, 60, 115
monograph, call numbers for, 116
statement, in collation, 60–61
Signature, definition, 57
Standard for Descriptive Cataloging of Government Scientific and Technical Reports, 19–20
Studies of Descriptive Cataloging, xviii, 13, 49, 52, 54, 57, 58
Subject heading, 65–95
alphabetico-classed catalog, 67–68, 84–87
books on, xix–xx
codes for, 20
compound, 66, 70–71
direct and specific, 69–71
lists, xix, 20, 82–84, 117
non-subject heading, 94–95
noun approach, 87–94
others, 91–94
Prevost, 88–90
Schwartz and Cutter, 87–88
objectives, 66–67, 79–81, 139–40
specific, 66, 67–71, 74–75, 113
subdivision, 66, 71–79
Cutter, 71–73
duplicate entry, 78–79

Haykin, 73–75, 77–78
  persons, 75–76
  places, 76–78
syndetic approach, 66, 79–81
uniform, 67, 140

Title
  main entry under, 45–46
  of periodicals, changed, 115
  of serials, changed, 37–38
  transcription, 51–53
  uniform, 32–33, 54–55, 140
Title entry
  for anonymous works, 32–33

books on, xvii–xix
as main entry, 44–46
objectives, 139–40
for serials, 37–40
Tracing, on catalog card, 62

Unit card, 45
Universal Decimal Classification, 135–37

Vatican Code, xviii, 13–14, 139

Wilson, H. W., Company, 148